# A BOY
# AT THE FOUR CORNERS

---

**Looking into Small-town America in its Prime**

**Bernard Ryan, Jr.**

AUTHOR'S NOTE: Some portions of this book have been published previously in *Air & Space Smithsonian*, *Atlantic Flyer*, *Heritage Villager*, and *Kent Quarterly*.

Other books by Bernard Ryan, Jr.

The Poodle at The Poodle
Tyler's Titanic
The Wright Brothers: Inventors of the Airplane
The Poisoned Life of Mrs. Maybrick
Jeffrey Bezos: Business Executive & Founder of
Amazon.com
Warren Buffett: Capitalist
Jimmy Carter: U.S. President
Hillary Rodham Clinton: First Lady & U.S. Senator
Stephen Hawking: Physicist and Cosmologist
Condoleezza Rice: Secretary of State
Community Service for Teens (8 vols)
Helping Your Child Start School
Simple Ways to Help Your Kids Become Dollar-Smart (with
Elizabeth Lewin)
Advertising for a Small Business Made Simple
So You Want to Go into Journalism (with Leonard Eames
Ryan)
So You Want to Go into Advertising

ISBN 1441426574   EAN-13 9781441426754

Bernard Ryan, Jr.
219 B Heritage Village
Southbury, Connecticut 06488
www.bernardryanjr.com
bernryan@snet.net

This book is lovingly dedicated

to my wife

Jean Bramwell Ryan

to my brothers and sisters

Priscilla Marbury Ryan

Hewitt Fitts Ryan

Valorie Vigil Ryan

Leonard Eames Ryan

Ann Allen-Ryan

and to the memory of my brother

William Fitts Ryan

because they have been there.

# Contents

## Illustrations

## Preface

There is nothing chronological about memory. It knows few dates. It weaves and wobbles back and forth through any given period – most so when it deals with boyhood, a great box into which one memory after another has tumbled or has been tossed, and in which the memories scramble around, seek relationships, compete for share of mind.

Sometimes we can find a key to that box, a way to sort and sift the memories, hold them, keep them clear. My key is The Four Corners – the downtown business section of the small town in Western New York State in which I spent my boyhood. Because that box of memories is always present, it speaks to me in the historic present tense.

– B.R. Jr.

# 1

## "Your Dad Knows You're Buying This Hatchet?"

When I think of small towns, I think of my boyhood in Albion. A Western New York town up in the far northwestern corner of the state, Albion set itself down on both sides of the Erie Canal back in the early 19th century when the canal was a-building. I cannot think of Albion without thinking of the canal. Stand with me now at the Main Street bridge over the canal, and I'll take you on a trip through town simply by strolling around The Four Corners – The Four Corners of my boyhood.

Imagine Main Street and Bank Street as a plus sign, Main running north and south, Bank running east and west. Downtown Albion – its business district – comprises the four blocks that make up this plus sign: a block of North Main, a block of South Main (after Bank crosses Main), a block of East Bank, and a block of West Bank (after Main crosses Bank).

As you stand with me now at the canal, our backs are to the bridge and Main Street lies before us to the south. We're elevated a bit – maybe six feet above the level of the sidewalks in front of the stores – because the bridge sits up on the shoulders of the canal, with the street ramping up to it. We can see the breadth of

Main Street. It is so wide that cars – mostly Fords and Chevys, with a scattering of `Model A's and even a few Model T's – are parked angled in to the curb. Even with that angled parking, winter plowing finds a giant ridge of snow built up down the center of Main Street, creating a boulevard. A block south, a traffic light stands on a pedestal in the center of the Main-and-Bank intersection.

The canal is quiet now. No tugboat pulling a string of barges can be seen off to the right, where the canal bends gently toward the southwest, a broad ripple of silver under the heavy gray Western New York sky. Out there, perhaps five hundred feet away, the little gray boat of the barge lamp lighter is tied up in its place, just where the squarish poured concrete canal edge, built so bargemen stopping in town can moor and step ashore, yields to the rubble embankment that guides the canal across the state. We'll come back to the canal when a barge toots for the Main Street bridge to rise and let it through.

Almost without exception, the buildings at The Four Corners stand three stories high, mostly built of heavy reddish-brown sandstone, a few of brick. The first on the right, as we step down the broad concrete steps (with their heavy black pipe-iron railing) from bridge level, contains Flickinger's Red-and-White Store, the first of six or seven grocery stores we'll see in The Four Corners. The only thing we ever buy from Flickinger's is my wagon, and I buy it myself. It is in the window, with a $4.00 price tag on it – red disk wheels, varnished wooden two-slat side rails that you lift in and out of shiny black brackets. I go in (I'm seven or eight, at most) and Mr. Flickinger (tall and bald, white shirt, black bow tie, white apron tied 'round his waist, sleeve garters, but Flickinger is not his name – the store is one of a chain, and we all

11

call him Mr. Flickinger) says he'll have to put one together. I can stop in after school and he'll have it ready. And so I do, happily pulling my new wagon all the way home – the mile or so down Main Street to the north. There I soon learn how to kneel on my right knee in the wagon (with the left side rail removed) and, with my left foot, push away the ground beneath me while my left hand grasps the wagon's gunwale to keep me balanced and my right hand steers the stick handle. So I zoom back and forth on the long veranda that surrounds the front and side of our big brick Victorian house or speed along the gravelly driveway that loops from Main Street around behind the house and back to Main Street.

"Mr. Flickinger" and his store disappear soon after I get my wagon, probably the victim of the Depression and of the competitive glut of grocery stores downtown. Nobody in my boyhood talks about "the depression." That's a term applied in retrospect. We know people who have tough times, lose businesses, commit suicide, but my pals and my parents never refer to "the depression."

Neidert & McKenna's Meat Market replaces Flickinger's Red and White Store. My mother buys meat there now and then, but mostly she gets beef and Sunday leg of lamb at the A and P up the block. Neidert & McKenna's lasts a year or two until Joe McKenna is appointed postmaster. Mr. McKenna is one of those men who has a single vertical furrow in his brow, a scowl furrow exactly between his heavy dark eyebrows and right in line with the part in the center of his black hair. But he has a sort of permanent grin down below, his ruddy cheeks pulled back with his smile lines. And of course the white shirt, black bow tie, apron tied at the waist. His partner, George Neidert, continues as a professional meat cutter for many years.

12

After Neidert & McKenna's, in that first store beside the canal, comes Joe Achilles and used furniture. Joe dresses for business. Suit, colored shirt, tie. A short man, kind of paunchy. Thinning gray hair, when he takes off his hat. Glasses sliding down his nose. Cigar. But Joe isn't a cigar chomper. He is a cigar gesturer. He doesn't clamp his cigar in the corner of his mouth and talk around it. He clamps it between his forefinger and second finger, either hand, and uses it as a pointer to emphasize his message.

Joe Achilles is the Albion philosopher of the 1930's. He uses two media to get his message out. The first is the sidewalk in front of his store. Six months of the year, May to October, you find an old wicker chair, from Joe's used-furniture stock, sitting on the sidewalk – with Joe Achilles sitting in it. In hot summer weather, his hat is a straw, his jacket is off, his shirt is a colorful plaid, his suspenders hang listlessly from his shoulders down across his paunch to his pants tops. Joe's chair is not where you would expect it to be, up against the storefront. It is out across the sidewalk, at the curb. For a sensible reason: so he can put his feet up on the front bumper of whatever automobile happens to be parked there while he reads *The New York Times* and all the Buffalo and Rochester papers. From that position, and usually with his gray whiskers shaved only every third or fourth day, Joe dispenses wise comment to passersby, most of whom he knows on a first-name basis. My Dad frequently comes home to lunch or dinner saying, "Well, you should hear Joe Achilles on the subject of so-and-so. He sees what's going on."

Joe's other medium is his column. For the *Orleans American* Joe writes a column under the pen name Argus. I don't know how many people in town know that

Argus is Joe Achilles. The column is short – usually about five or six column inches. Always on the front page, usually in the lower left or right corner. Pithy. What we'd call a zap today, on some current national issue.

Wahl's Bakery stands next door to Joe Achilles's store. Fall, winter or spring, it smells good when I walk by on the way to and from school. On some Sundays after church, but not every Sunday, Dad stops in at Wahl's to buy sweet rolls – big, heavy cinnamon-and-sugar rolls that come in a block of a dozen.

And next door to Wahl's is Hank Hudson's. Hank Hudson's, the bicycle and auto accessories store to end all bike-and-auto stores. Even the building is different. Only two stories high. With the entire storefront painted a solid blood red. Flickinger's is white with black trim. Wahl's is solid white. Hank Hudson's: red red. To go into Flickinger's, you climb two steps. To go into Wahl's, you climb two steps. To go into Hank Hudson's, you walk right in at sidewalk level. But first you stop at the window. In fact, you stop at the window every day, going to and from school, to see what's new and different. And there it all is: red reflectors and amber reflectors, to put on your car's license plates or your bike's fender, jackknives, flashlights, hunting knives, axes, bicycle pumps, hatchets, shotguns, fire extinguishers, lanterns, sterno stoves, work gloves, .22 rifles, at least one bicycle, a couple of bike tires, a couple of auto tires, a Boy Scout mess kit and canteen and knapsack in World War I khaki canvas, and you name it, it's there.

Inside, Hank Hudson's is low-ceilinged. Straight ahead, to the rear, is a big open area. It is big enough so an automobile can drive right in from the rear, through the big double door that stands open in summer weather, letting in great splashes of

14

afternoon sunlight from the west – light as bright as Hank Hudson's smile and the shine of his almost entirely bald head.

But there is seldom a car in that open area inside the big door. Usually two or three bicycles are there in various states of repair, set upside down on their seats and handlebars with wheels removed and tires being repaired or replaced. And to the right, in the relative darkness away from the bright light of the big open doors, is the big display case and countertop. Here Hank Hudson shows me and my brother Bill, whose idea it is to buy a hatchet, his entire line: small lightweight hatchets, big hefty hatchets. Bill decides on a two-dollar hatchet – light, wieldy. Hank Hudson leans down, his elbows on the countertop, and hunches toward us, speaking just above a whisper: "Your Dad knows you're buying this hatchet?"

Bill nods. He carries the hatchet home.

The house in Albion *circa* 1966. Photo by Bernard Ryan, Jr.

## 2

### "When You Tip to the Right, Turn to the Right."

When I'm 10 years old, I announce that I wish I had a bike. Dad goes with me to Hank Hudson's. We pick out a full-size, bright blue bike. Dad pays Hank Hudson twenty dollars and I push the bike out onto the sidewalk, off the curb, up the ramp onto the bridge, across the bridge, and down the hill on the other side, then the mile down the Main Street sidewalk and home. I don't yet know how to ride a bike.

The big wide veranda that crosses the front of our house and then goes down the south side has a wide six-step stair at each end. Every afternoon after school, I push my new bike around from the garage out behind the house to the side steps. From the bottom step, I swing aboard, push off headed across our side yard, pedal 10 or 20 feet, and flop over. I cannot get the hang of it. After a few days, my brother Bill, who is 18 months older but does not yet have a bike, borrows mine to ride to school. He has already learned to ride Tommy Heard's bike. When he comes home, I go at it again. My knees and elbows are battered.

Two weeks go by, Bill riding my bike to school, me not riding across the side yard. Then one day Walter Monacelli is mowing the lawn. Walter is high-school age. His mowing price is 25 cents an hour. When it looks like rain, Walter usually stops mowing and takes off for home, and when he comes back Mama says, "Walter, you're not made of sugar. You won't melt in the rain."

Today Walter sees me push off from the side steps, roll a few feet, and flop over. He stops mowing and calls over to me. "It's easy. When you tip to the right, turn to the right. When you tip to the left, turn to the left."

I get back on, push off, and ride across the side yard, around to the left across the front yard, onto the north driveway, back around behind the house, out the south driveway, back across the side yard, around the house altogether three times without stopping, and to school the next morning.

From then on, Bill doesn't get another chance to ride my bike to school. Soon Dad takes Bill in to Hank Hudson's and Bill gets his own bike – blue like mine, but a double-bar bike. Its frame has two rods, rather than one, between the seat post and the steering post, and the handlebars have a straight connecting rod attached just ahead of the handgrips. This significant difference between my bike and Bill's is attributed by my parents to Bill's being older.

Now I'm all over town on my bike – up to Tom McNall's on South Main (Tom's older brother, Burt, also has a double-bar bike, but his has balloon tires), over to Richard Gminski's on Linwood Avenue.

One day I'm nearly home from school, riding along on the sidewalk and just in front of the Dibley house. A boy who is younger than I (he's probably seven or eight, and I'm probably ten or eleven) is playing with an automobile tire in the front yard. I recognize him as a visiting nephew of the Dibleys. As I roll by about ten feet from him, he suddenly rolls the car tire at me. It hits my front wheel. I fly over the handlebars, tumbling onto the lawn – luckily not onto the concrete walk. I jump up, pick up my bike and see that the front fender is twisted and crumpled. I grab the kid by the arm. Why he's hanging around I don't know. I tell him he's going to have to pay for this. He stares up at me, wordless. I let him go, and push my bike the last 1,000 feet home. I can't ride it, because the twisted fender hits the bike frame when I turn the handlebars. Next day, I push it up Main Street and over the bridge to Hank Hudson's. The day after that, I stop by to pick it up. Hank has smoothed out the fender, good as new, for three dollars. Years later, it dawns on me that he didn't smooth it out, he installed a new fender.

Another time when I'm passing the Dibleys', I hear a loud snorting, snuffling and gurgling sound. I look across the lawn at their front porch. Behind the banisters, face up, flat on his back, lies their boarder, Albert Coyle. His body is quivering, rigid. His heavy breathing is making the noise. Dad has told me that Albert has epileptic fits. That's why he has so many scars on his face, Dad says – sometimes he just falls flat on his face, right on the sidewalk.

I don't know what to do. Should I knock on the door, see if anybody's home, tell them Albert is lying there having a fit?  When Dad told me about Albert falling on his face, I said, "Well, what happens then?" Dad said, "It passes. And he goes along. Sometimes it doesn't happen again for months."

I pedal on my way. The next time I see Albert Coyle, he is in church, dressed in his suit, white shirt, tie. A year or so later, Dad comes home and says, "Well, the Dibleys' star boarder, Albert Coyle, is leaving town. Going to North Carolina." Albert has placed a mail-order ad for a bride, and a woman in North Carolina has taken him up on it – if he'll come there. I find myself wondering if he sent a picture, and if it showed him in weekday dress – needing a comb and a shave, no tie, rumpled white shirt, baggy pants hanging by suspenders and draped below his paunch, cuffs bunched over his shoes and wearing through at the heels – or if it showed his Sunday best. I never see Albert again, but I remember his always hoarse voice and the sound of his fit.

# 3

## "This Is The Original Paris Garter."

Next door to Hank Hudson's is E. J. Ross Hardware. This is a big double store, occupying two storefronts (battleship gray on the outside), with two front doors, separated by a long stretch of display window, up two steps from the sidewalk. It's a pots-and-pans hardware store, selling all kinds of kitchen utensils, ironing boards, percolators, electric irons, vacuum cleaners, brooms and dustpans, cups and saucers and other china – everything that would be called "housewares" in a department store. Mr. Ross is a big man, bald on top, fringe of salt-and-pepper hair, wire-framed glasses, moustache, blue shirt, dark gray cardigan sweater that always hangs open. His son, Derek, is one of my school pals.

After E. J. Ross Hardware is a narrow store at the corner of Beaver Alley, a slim parting of the storefronts that runs west and is scarcely wide enough to let two cars pass. This store has no name. No sign hangs above the short display window or over the door. Inside are yard goods, thread, yarn, needles, buttons. You walk in at sidewalk level through a door set into the corner at a 45-degree angle, in effect cutting off the ground-level corner of the store. To hold up the upstairs corner, a post stands in front of the door. Post and storefront are painted – dark green.

Beaver Alley is somber. Looking westward from the corner, you see on the left a succession of abandoned, boarded-up storefronts in a high wall of rough native stone. A block away, a second-floor enclosed bridge crosses the alley to connect with a big square windowless building. On the right is an open space, a parking lot, at the rear of the little green yard-goods store. The windowless building on the far right – a gambrel-roofed wooden building – is a millwork. When you drive through Beaver Alley, you hear the high-pitched screech of big saws, the whir of lathes, and from a stove-pipe that sticks out horizontally from high up in the wall, then points toward the ground, you see a steady blast of sawdust and shavings that pile up in a mound eight or ten feet high. The mound disappears every couple of weeks. You never see anybody. No trucks coming and going. No workers heaving lumber in or newel posts out. Dad has no dealings with anyone there. It's as if the mill just screeches and whirs and breathes sawdust all by itself.

Florence Budd seems to belong to Beaver Alley. Florence Budd ranges up and down Main Street pulling a wagon much like mine from Flickinger's, except that hers is years older and more beat-up and is loaded with flotsam and jetsam she has picked up on the street – broken umbrellas, salvageable cardboard boxes that might come in handy some day, a lost glove, bits of rag and cord. Florence wears wire-frame glasses down at the end of her nose. She is wrapped in a cape-like olive drab something – a garment – that may have been made from an abandoned U.S. Army blanket from the Great War. It almost entirely covers her, and reaches to her ankles.

I have no idea where Florence Budd lives, but she uses Beaver Alley for her entrances and exits on Main Street – except on the day when a circus comes to the Fair Grounds, out West State Street. They put on a parade through town, and they have one elephant. Florence Budd, her wagon emptied of its usual collection, follows the elephant along the parade route and scoops up the elephant droppings, announcing to whoever is listening on either curbside that there is nothing like elephant manure for growing immense cabbages in her garden. From this event I gain the impression that she has a home somewhere up near the Fair Grounds.

On the other corner of Beaver Alley and Main Street stands the Pratt Building, an 1880's edifice of Medina sandstone standing three stories tall. At street level are two stores. The first, at the corner, offers dinette sets – chunky maple tables and chairs, or shiny chrome-plated bent pipe legs with caned seats and backs. They sit before columns of rolled linoleum flooring. I sense depression – mental, not economic – when I walk by that store.

But next to it, at the center of the Pratt Building, is a wide flight of steps pushing upward into the building. They are interrupted about eight steps up, well back into the building, by a double door that always stands open in warm weather so you can see up to the top of the stairs. On the risers are two wide signs, one for "Falconio – Dry Cleaning – Tailoring," the other for "Schwartz – Cleaning, Pressing, Tailoring."

Don't ask me how Marcus Schwartz and Charlie Falconio managed to land their separate and competing businesses on the same second floor of the Pratt

Building. Maybe it's good for business. They say shoe stores like to be within half a block of other shoe stores.

Dad takes any clothing that needs repair to Marcus Schwartz. The tailor sits at a work table facing the tall windows that look out on Main Street. He is a little man atop a stool, hunched forward, his jaw jutting out, stretched out from his white shirt collar, his curly gray hair in ringlets down over the back of the collar. His eyes are in a permanent squint. When he appears outdoors, summer or winter, he wears a black hat, brim up all the way around.

Marcus Schwartz is always glad to see us. He sets down his scissors or his needle and turns to greet us. "Boys, how are you? How is school?"

Across the hall is Charlie Falconio. His door is always open, and we can see him in there – a tall man, not hunched over like Marcus Schwartz. Curly gray hair, balding at the temples. Glasses. His son Chuck is a year behind me in school, destined to become the Harry James of the high school band and then a star trumpeter in U.S. Army bands all through World War II. The Falconios live on Erie Street, a single block off Main Street   north of the canal, about half way to our house. Erie is overflowing with kids – more children than any other street in town. They're all over the place. When you drive through the block, you interrupt a dozen games of hopscotch, scrub baseball, jump rope.

Between Marcus Schwartz's and Charlie Falconio's is the stair going up to the third floor. That floor is condemned, Dad says – too old, dangerous, floorboards maybe rotted. What's up there? The Pratt Opera House. A complete theatre. Plush velvet curtains, long sloping floor that goes down into the rear of the building (behind

24

the long, high, rough-stone wall above the abandoned store-fronts of Beaver Alley), genuine stage and fly-loft. Out of business since the Rialto movie theatre was built, up hill on Main, the other side of Bank, in the early '20's.

Here were Dad's early appearances on the stage, after he had graduated from high school at the age of 15 and while he was taking two successive years of "P.G." – post-graduate high school work – followed by two years of working in Ramsdale and Church's law office for 50 cents a week. That was before he went to Albany Law School and was admitted to the bar and then decided to try the stage and landed a job in Jessie Bonestell's traveling stock company when she came through Buffalo in 1912 (the company included a young leading man named William Powell).


The store on the south side of the Pratt Building stairway is Sammet's haberdashery. This is where Dad buys his new boater – every May. Dad believes in straw hats from Memorial Day to Labor Day, then back to felt. Dad buys his suits in Rochester, at the Hickey-Freeman factory. But socks, ties, maybe even shirts come from Sammet's, where Herman Nuremberg, the proprietor, is usually standing just inside the door waiting to greet you.

One day, Dad needs new garters. Herman sells him a pair. "This is the original Paris garter," he says as he shows a pair to Dad, "top notch." Dad takes them home, puts them on. His socks fall down. The elastic in the garters is dead (and this is long before socks themselves have elastic inside). Dad takes them back. "Herman," he says, "you're right. This *is* the original Paris garter."

25

Maybe tired merchandise is a symptom of the Depression. Next door to Sammet's is Landauer & Strauss, a big dry-goods and ready-to-wear store for ladies. Like E.J. Ross Hardware, it occupies two storefronts and has two entrance doors. The paint on Landauer's storefront is a warm butterscotch color, and the store name runs across the full width of the two fronts, high above them, on one of those signs made with rounded cutout letters, butterscotch on black and set deep into a frame.

You never know whether Jakey Landauer will be standing behind the north door or the south door, but you always know his nose will be pressed against the glass as he peers into Main Street. There he smiles, waves, nods, to all who pass by, including me.

Jakey has been mayor of Albion longer than anyone can remember. He is a small man, the only man in Albion who wears pince-nez spectacles. His hair is gray, sleeked straight back behind his ears. He seems to have no shoulders – his arms hang somehow from the sloping shape below his neck. His big black Packard – so big it has two spare tires, one sunk into each front fender, just behind the front wheels and forward of the front doors – is always parked right in front of the store. When you see Jakey Landauer at the wheel of the Packard, he is wearing a black homburg, summer or winter, and he is leaning forward as if something is propping him up as he peers intently ahead.

One day, Marguerite Harding decides to make dresses for Joan, one of my schoolmates, whose name is pronounced Joanne despite its spelling. She buys yards of material from bolts at Landauer's, cuts shapes from patterns, sews by the hour. Joan is outfitted for months of schooldays to come. But the first washing opens

26

seams. Buttons pull out. The fabric tears at a touch. The material is like the original Paris garter from Sammet's. It sat in the store for too many years before Mrs. Harding came in.

**4**

**"I'll Take Two."  "I'll Take Fifty."**

Next door to Landauer's stands The Greek's. This is the soda fountain, the candy store, the popcorn stand. There is no sign overhead, but the popcorn machine is always outside the door, on the landing one step up from the sidewalk. The fake sundaes are in the windows – rich chocolate sauce on vanilla ice cream, topped by whipped cream and chocolate sprinkles and a cherry, a banana split in all its glory, even a tall soda glass (the kind of glass with curvy horizontal layers, as if it belongs to The Michelin Man). They look delicious, if you don't look closely enough to see their specks of soot. And, if he is not busy, Gus Theodorakis himself is standing in the open door, just behind the popcorn machine. Gus is a big man, with his hands in his pockets behind his broad white apron, his black bow tie on his white shirt but partly tucked under his double chin, his heavy moustache in a grin and his eyes just two smiling dark slits behind his steel-framed spectacles.

The Greek's storefront is painted red. So is the A & P next door. It has the standard "The Great Atlantic & Pacific Tea Co." sign above, and inside it is a long, narrow shop that expands, at the rear, into an L shape, spreading to the right behind

The Greek's. This A & P is the best meat market in town. Mr. Miller is the butcher, father of my schoolmate Marilyn Miller. When Mama sends us in to buy ground round, she always says, "Be sure they put it through the grinder twice." Maybe that's why her hamburgers taste better than anybody else's.

Beside the A & P is Hawks's Rexall Drugstore. The paint is gray. The door is right at sidewalk level. Inside is the classic early 20th century American pharmacy: on the right, two long display cases with slanting glass fronts, full of bath salts, perfumes, after shaves, lipsticks, compacts, powders. On the left, wall cabinets loaded with toothpaste, aspirin, first-aid equipment, brushes, combs, cough syrup. Over all this Min Hawks presides. She is tall and skinny. Hair tucked up above her ears, rouge on her cheeks like a painted doll, beige sweater and tweedy beige skirt under a hip-length white jacket with short sleeves, so her sweater arms show below them. Mrs. Hawks wears steel-rimmed glasses, smiles a lot, talks through her nose in a clipped, high-pitched way. She dispenses horehound drops by the pound in a plain white bag.

On the right at the rear stands the marble-topped soda fountain, with six or eight ice-cream-parlor stools with twisted wire legs. In the area before the fountain are four or five small round tables with their ice-cream-parlor chairs. Here the merchants amble in from Main and Bank streets for their lunches or their late afternoon cokes, usually served by Harold Hawks, who steps over to the soda fountain from his stand behind the prescription counter that runs across the rear of the store. Ray Fuller is his best customer. Ray is down from his law office, upstairs on East Bank, just off Main Street, for morning coffee, noontime sandwich, four o'clock coke. Dad says Ray tells all his clients' business at Harold Hawks's, wintertimes, anyway, when it's too cold to stand for long on the sidewalk out front and tell it. Ray is entirely bald, long narrow head, long, long face with strong jaw and long yellow teeth, deep smile lines. He's tall and thin and hunched over. In later years, when they put parking meters up and down Main Street, he finds them handy to hang onto and hunch over while he talks with Dad about his clients.

Harold Hawks is the opposite of his wife in just about every way. He's paunchy, heavy-set, hoarse of voice. His shirt cuffs are open, rolled back a turn or two half way to his elbows. His head is balding, completely round (almost a perfect ball shape), his face round, his wire-framed glasses creasing the flesh below his temples. Harold closes the store at one o'clock every Wednesday. By two o'clock, he is on the golf course over at Batavia, 18 miles away.

He has strong opinions. When Mama's novel, *Mother of the Groom*, is published, the publisher's rep comes into town looking for a bookstore and is astonished to find none. Mama advises him that the drugstores in town carry some books. He calls on Harold Hawks, gives him his pitch. Harold looks at him without enthusiasm, says, "I'll take two." Across Main Street, Harold's competitor, Alice Sayles, says, "I'll take 50," sells them all, and repeats the order. She is aptly named.

Mystery: Harold and Min Hawks have no children. I can never understand this. They live on Erie Street, second house from Main Street, on the left. Erie is the one-block-long street of kids. Every house hugs a big family. Except the Hawks's. What are they doing there? How can they live there and not have kids?

Next door, at the corner of Main and Bank, is the bank. The Orleans Trust Company. Later the Marine Midland. The building looks like a bank: It is stone, a grayish off-white in color, with two small windows (one on each side of the center door) facing Main Street. If you stand back and look up, you see that the bank building includes Hawks's drugstore, for the stone facing goes up all three floors and covers the floors above Hawks's. This is worth knowing only when you find, some years later, that the bank has expanded into the Hawks space and Harold and Min Hawks have been forced to move. They wind up down Main Street at the corner of Beaver Alley, replacing the nameless notions-and-yarn-and-sewing-materials store with the post in front of the corner door.

The president of the bank is Tom Heard. He sits in the front corner of the bank, his back right at Main and Bank, looking westward down the row of teller's cages that back up to Bank Street. Mr. Heard is tall, with thick black hair parted in the center of his head – a serious looking man, like a banker should be. He's the father of my brother Bill's best pal, Tommy Heard, and of Dick, who is in my grade in school, and of Pete and Donald. When *Life* magazine is launched, Mr. Heard saves every issue. Years and years later, when the magazine is suspended by Time Inc., he has the complete set. During World War I, the story goes, Mr. Heard was a spy for the American Expeditionary Force, and he brought home a cane he used that is actually a concealed sword.

Bill and Tommy build a clubhouse in our yard, just across the driveway from our front door. They make it from odds and ends of lumber that are lying around after Dad has our garage built, back across the driveway from our kitchen door. Sometimes they let me come into the clubhouse, if I am willing to be "the servant." One day we are in the clubhouse. Bill knows that Mama has made cookies. I am sent to the

31

kitchen to get some. Mama wants to know why Bill and Tommy didn't come in to get cookies. "I'll take them some," I say. "I'm the servant."

"Well, I guess not!" says Mama, heading for the kitchen door and a confrontation at the clubhouse. I stop her, howling, "But I *want* to be the servant!"

She tells that one for years.

Dick Heard comes to all my birthday parties. He can be depended on to spill his cocoa. But when World War II gets under way and Dick goes up to the Army Air Corps induction center at Niagara Falls and takes the coordination test, he gets the highest mark they've ever seen. One day in fourth grade, when Dick can't settle down in class, our teacher, Mrs. Paine, loses her temper, stuffs him – knees against chin – into the big green metal wastebasket in the corner near her desk, tips it on its side, and rolls him out the door, across the hall, and off down the stairway to the floor below.

At the center of the bank building, between the Hawks Drugstore and the bank, is a narrow door with a stairway behind it (not a generous double door and wide stair, like the Pratt Building's). It leads to The Town Club.

I don't know much about The Town Club. Mama and Dad are not members. It is a mysterious place where people drink and play poker and dance. Sometimes on a Saturday night, if you stroll down Main Street when you come out of the movies, you hear loud music at Main and Bank. You don't quite know where it is coming from. It is coming from The Town Club.

Around the corner from the bank, down Bank Street to the west, the building is a long brick wall, painted the same gray off-white as the front of the building on Main Street. First behind the bank is a liquor store, dark and narrow. Next is a dry-cleaner's. We patronize neither. But the dry-cleaning proprietor is a highly visible guy, always in and out, putting shirt boxes and suits and dresses on hangers into his truck. He wears a gray fedora, brim always turned up in front. Steel-framed glasses that sink into a permanent crease across the bridge of his nose. Business suit, white shirt, tie. He walks like a duck, toes turned out widely. Years later, when television puts Ed Wynn in my living room, I realize that in my childhood I watched him load his dry-cleaner truck countless times.

Marsh's Hardware. This is a big, wide-open store – twice the width of the liquor store and the dry-cleaner's put together. The ceiling is high, so high there is room for a balcony across the full width of the rear of the store. The cashier and desk workers are up there. Marsh's is a genuine hardware store, much more so than E. J. Ross's, which is really a housewares store. Marsh's is where the professionals – the plumbers, the electricians, the builders – come to get parts.

And Marsh's is where Dick Heard goes to work when he comes home from the war in 1946. It is the job he retires from in 1989. In between, sometime in the 1960's, my family and I are visiting Albion and we stop in a supermarket. Half way down one aisle, I say something to my wife. A voice from the next aisle calls out my name. It is Dick Heard, who has recognized my voice after more than 20 years.

Beyond Marsh's on Bank Street is an open lot. In it stands a tall elm tree – the closest tree to The Four Corners. Then, at the corner of Liberty Street, is Coffey Brothers Gulf. Francis, Tom, and Ted Coffey run a major gas station, repair shop, and fuel-oil business. Their entire building – with the pump islands parallel to Bank Street, two service bays facing Bank, a long  garage with three or four service bays facing Liberty – all the walls and trim are painted orange to match the orange of the Gulf signs.

Coffey Brothers keep the two big tanks in our cellar filled with oil. The tanks are big – two 500 gallon tanks – because sometimes when the snow drifts into our driveway it is a week or more before they could get a truck in to refill them.

One day I'm walking home from school. I'm nearly home, already past the Dibleys', just about at the town line, where the red-brick pavement of Main Street changes to the Macadam of route 98 and the American Legion Sheret Post No. 35 sign says, "Albion – Drive Slowly, We Love Our Children," when I see a car coming toward me that looks like our Chevy. It looks like our Chevy except that the front grill and bumper and headlights and fenders and wheels and even the tires are green. As it passes me it is driving anything but slowly, and I recognize Ted Coffey at the wheel. At the same time, I say to myself that that looks like the same color green that is being put on our kitchen cabinets this week.

It is not only the same color. It is the same paint. Mama tells me that she got all ready to drive in to Rochester, went to the garage, and found my little brothers, Hewitt and Leonard, who are about five and three years old – and the car – all covered with green paint. The only thing she could think of to do was call Ted Coffey.

They work into the evening and get most of it off, using gasoline as the paint remover. But when Sam Shelp, the Chevy dealer, takes the car in trade a couple of years later, you can still find traces of green paint deep in the crevices.

On the south side of West Bank Street, at the corner of Liberty, is Joe Dibley's blacksmith barn. Like all the other buildings in The Four Corners business section, it dates from long before the automobile – a big three-story barn with weathered dark gray board siding that shows no sign of paint, just like any barn on a farm. When you walk by in weather warm enough for the big sliding door to be open, you can see farm implements that are in for repair: harrows, plows, cultivators, maybe even a side-delivery rake. And you can see the acetylene tanks standing ready for whatever welding job is next.

Both Joe Dibley and his father (grandfather of Don Dibley, who is older than my brother Bill) wear shirts with detachable collars, and the collars are detached. A brass collar-button hangs in the buttonhole below each Dibley's Adam's apple. In warm weather, both wear vests that hang open over the dirty white shirts above baggy trousers. Old Mr. Dibley has tufts of reddish and graying hair above his ears, thin hair on top, and a heavy paunch down below. Joe Dibley's hair is darker and thicker, but he's balding at the temples. Both shave now and then. Both smoke cigars. Unlike Jakey Landauer or Herman Nuremberg or Derek Ross's father, they don't smile or say hello when you walk by their business place. They just look at you, if they are near the door. If they are not near the door, you can't see them anyway, for the blacksmith shop always seems dark and dingy unless they are welding and the acetylene torch is flashing brightly and showering sparks. Then you want to stand in the doorway and watch Joe Dibley hunched over whatever rig he is fixing, his wide black mask dropped down over his face, his black leather apron protecting his collarless shirt and open vest and baggy pants.

Slowly, over the years when I am in school, the Dibley welding operation moves from the barn on West Bank Street to the small barn that stands just behind the Dibley house (the house where the kid who was visiting rolled the tire into my bike, and where I saw Albert Coyle stretched out on the porch floor having a fit). Acetylene tanks and more and more pieces of scrap iron and odd items to be fixed appear in the Dibley back yard. Old Mr. Dibley spends most of the day rocking in a chair on the front porch. Joe Dibley rocks sometimes, too, in open vest and collarless shirt. They look at me as I go by. I try not to look at them. Now the barn door on West Bank is never open.

## 5

## "How Old Is This Pup?"

Moving back toward Main Street from the Dibleys' barn, you see a small open space. It fills up with weeds in the summertime. It is not a parking lot. It is just a small vacant lot. Next is the rear of the building that faces Main at the corner of Bank. Here are two narrow doors in the gray painted brick wall. One is the back door of Wilcox Hardware, with a small sign above it saying so. The other has no sign. It opens on the steep narrow stairway to the home of Doc Hedges.

We take Sambo to Doc Hedges. Sambo is the puppy that Dad buys for me late one afternoon – just at dusk, with the sun already down beyond the trees to the west – when we are visiting a farmer somewhere out West State Street beyond the Gaines Basin Road. Dad is the farmer's lawyer on some small problem or other, and as they finish talking and are strolling back to the car a frolicking bunch of mongrel puppies, all black and white, are underfoot. "Would you buy one?" asks the farmer.

"How much?" says Dad.

"A dollar."

37

We take Sambo home with us. He is entirely black, except for a dash of white in the center of his chest. And he is my dog. Bill already has a dog – Prince, part Collie, part something else. Prince looks like a small Collie, except that his nose has a dip in it just below his eyes, unlike a purebred Collie's absolutely straight nose.

For two days, Sambo won't eat whatever Mama puts before him. "We'll take him to Doc Hedges," says Dad.

We go that evening. Doc Hedges is an old, old man. He wears a heavy tweed suit and a bow tie. He walks slowly, hunched over. Mrs. Hedges is in the kitchen, to the right at the rear of the apartment. She stands in the kitchen door and says hello, then goes back out of sight. She is old, too. Very old.

Doc Hedges smiles at me, pats my head, takes Sambo in his arms, gently pushes his mouth open, pats his head, slowly rubs his thumbs over Sambo's chest between his forelegs. "How old is this pup?" he says without looking up.

"Well, they told me four weeks," says Dad.

"Too young," says Doc Hedges. "Too young to leave home. Needs his mother. You leave him with us for a few days. I think we can get him going."

We go back in a week or so. This time we go to Doc Hedges's office, in a barn on Liberty Street, out behind the business block where Doc Hedges lives upstairs, and just up Liberty behind the Dibley barn. It is a big old drive barn from the days when a horse and carriage could be rented downtown. The floor is heavy broad planks, with room for six or eight carriages. To the rear are several stables standing open and empty. The wood of their walls is a glistening dark reddish brown. The walls are topped by vertical iron bars, black and twisted. The place smells like dry straw.

On the right is the office, where Doc Hedges and Sambo are waiting. The puppy looks twice as big as a week ago. He runs all around us, his tail wagging merrily. "Gave him a bottle," says Doc Hedges to Dad. "Kept him near the stove. He'll be all right."

He looks at me. "Tell your mother. Milk toast. Nice and warm. For another week. Every evening, about five o'clock. All right? Then he can have anything."

Sambo is the opposite of Prince in just about every way. He's maybe two thirds Prince's size – about a foot high. His coat is short and sleek. He never sheds. Overnight, he and Prince become pals, playing, chasing, sleeping together.

Sambo teaches me about dog communication. One day I'm sitting on the side porch and Sambo is lying near me at the top of the steps (the steps where I launched my tries at bike riding) with his paws hanging over the edge. He growls. I look up. A strange dog has come into the yard and is sniffing around the trees out at the end of the driveway. Sambo gets up and stands at the top of the steps. He barks loudly at the strange dog. The dog keeps on sniffing. He doesn't even look up. Sambo barks again, more vociferously. No response.

Sambo turns and runs to the rear of the porch, 12 or 15 feet away, facing away from the visitor. Now he barks an entirely different bark – more high-pitched, maybe an octave up the scale, and more staccato – toward the rear of the house.

Instantly I hear Prince barking, and within seconds a flash of brown and white comes hurtling around the corner of the house, barking furiously. Sambo flies down the steps, now resuming his first angry barking, and together he and Prince dispatch the offending stranger, who hurries out the driveway with his tail between his legs.

One day a couple of years later I get home from school. Mama has gone to Rochester to shop. Mrs. Claus, who moved into the upstairs back room a few weeks ago as our new cook, is in the kitchen. She has a handkerchief at her nose. Her cheeks glisten with tears. Sambo, she tells me, was hit by a car. Someone who stopped took him to Doctor Beebe. I ask if she called Doctor Beebe. "I couldn't," she says. "The poor little dog."

Doctor Beebe is the vet with the big house up on State Street, near Clinton. At the rear, at the end of a long driveway, is a large barn – his office and kennels. We have never gone to Dr. Beebe. I call him up, tell him who I am, ask about the little black dog that was hit. "Oh, he died," says Dr. Beebe flatly. I think of Doc Hedges gently rubbing Sambo's chest with his thumbs. I feel Doc Hedges patting me on the head. I can tell – Doctor Beebe would never do either of those things.

I find myself wondering whose car hit Sambo. Sambo never chased cars. He wasn't the kind of dog who made errors of timing or judgment. I say to myself, Was it the same man who hit Jiggs?

We had Jiggs before Prince or Sambo. He was an all white mongrel with a black ring around one eye. We named him for the central character in "Bringing Up Father" in the funny papers. Jiggs was frequently given a black eye by his wife, Maggie, who wielded a rolling pin.

I saw Jiggs get hit. I was on the side porch that time, too. He had been over at the Lettis farm, across the road, and was crossing home again when a Model A Ford, headed for town at high speed, hit him. He yelped, ran to the edge of the road, lay down and died. The driver screeched the brakes, backed up, turned in at our driveway. Mama heard the screech and came out onto the porch. The man who got out of the car said he was awfully sorry. He was late for an appointment in town with his dentist. Robert Lettis, who was probably 18 or 19, came out of their house, picked Jiggs up on a piece of burlap bag, carried him across our back field and deep into the evergreens, and buried him – we never knew just where.

A year or two later, I was riding my bike home from school. It was a clear autumn day, the sky an intense blue. I had passed the town line, moving from the red brick pavement to the macadam of the open road outside town. I was riding on the right side. Nearing home, already at the Lettis farm, I looked over my shoulder to see if any traffic was behind me. A car was just at the town line – plenty of time for me to turn left and cross the road into our south driveway. I turned.

A wild screech of brakes. Dust flying. A spinning, horrible noise. A Model A Ford beside me sideways, on my left. I cut to the right. The car spun more, its rear now toward me. It shot into the left-hand ditch and stopped. I got off my bike, pushed it across the road, stopped at the passenger side of the car. The window was open. "I'm sorry, mister," I said shakily.

Already he was putting the car in reverse, revving the engine. "It's okay," he said as the car started to move.

He backed out of the ditch as I recognized him. The man who killed Jiggs.

A long time later I understood. I had never before had to coordinate my crossing the road with the speed of a car that left the town line at 50 or 60 miles an hour. Jiggs had never had to coordinate his crossing with the speed of a car that was going to enter town at such speed. Was Sambo a third – three of us caught by the same speeder?

# 6

## "Look Who I Found in the Middle of the Road."

We are back at the corner of Main and Bank, looking south along the west side of Main. Here at the corner is the New York State Gas & Electric Company. The building is the same gray storefront as the long wall down Bank Street where Doc Hedges goes in and out. None of us ever goes in or out of the gas company headquarters. Its show windows display shiny new white gas ranges, the kind that stand on legs and put the oven and broiler up at waist height.

Next door is E. W. Wilcox Hardware. Bud Wilcox is a lifelong friend of Dad's. He played tennis regularly on the court Dad built on the north lawn of our house when he was a boy. Bud Wilcox's father built the hardware business, and it is the town's biggest and best. The store is wide and deep, L-shaped so it cuts to the right behind the gas company's corner store and comes out on Bank Street through the side door next to Doc Hedges's. Up front are counters and shelves loaded with all the things people buy at hardware stores all the time: nuts and bolts, screws, hinges, nails, paint, paintbrushes, masking tape, you-name-it – all the things that add up to

Dad's saying, "If people would just look around the house before they go down to the hardware store, the hardware stores would go out of business."

Farther back are the things the professionals come in for: stands of stovepipe, racks of electrical and plumbing parts and carpentry tools. Wilcox's is where I buy my first long-nosed pliers and the crosscut saw I still use today, more than 60 years later.

Bud Wilcox can move fast. Mama calls him one morning. "Bud, we need a fence." She is calling him five minutes after Earl Harding knocks on the door with my baby brother, Leonard, in his arms. "Harriet," he says, "look who I found in the middle of the road."

Leonard is crawling age. He is supposed to be on a blanket on the lawn, out in the sun absorbing vitamins to make up for some illness he had in the winter. The middle of the road – route 98 – is a long crawl from his blanket. Earl Harding, father of my schoolmate Joan, whose homemade dresses came apart, grows cherries in vast orchards on his father's farm a half mile north on 98.

Bud Wilcox's crew is there that afternoon, putting up a cyclone fence – steel posts and horizontal beams top and bottom, strong chain-link fencing, gates across both the north and south driveways. It stretches 200 feet or so all the way across the front of our property. It will last more than 50 years. In the spring, Mama has a barberry hedge put in in front of the fence. It grows up prickly and dense and reddish. You have to look to know a fence is behind it.

Bud Wilcox's wife, Elizabeth, is from Shreveport, Louisiana. They met when Bud was stationed down there in the Navy during The Great War. They live up on

South Main Street, almost at the town line at that end of Albion. Elizabeth's sister's husband, Fred Boone, is a Captain in the Navy – and a pilot. One day, just before lunchtime, a deafening roar sweeps over town, then comes back in the other direction. I dash outdoors, look up, see nothing but sky. Someone phones Mama. Fred Boone has just landed on the Moore farm.

We jump into the car, drive through town and up South Main. The Moore farm is the first outside the town line, only five or six houses beyond the Wilcoxes. Cars are pulling into the Moore driveway, hurrying past the barns into the big long open field that stretches to the east. There it is. It stands solidly, like a giant toy alone and proud in the center of a broad space that is all its own.

Cars park far back from it. People get out, walking slowly, studying it. Some seem a little sheepish, as if they know it is silly to drop everything and come running to see an airplane, yet knowing they *must* have a look. We get out. The ground is dusty dry, a field of stubble after the wheat has been harvested.

It is the Navy's Grumman fighter, the first carrier-based biplane with retractable landing gear. The wheels tuck up into the fat belly below the lower wing, fitting into round holes just their size and looking like great button emblems. The wings themselves, I know (for I'm a model-plane buff and I have illustrations clipped from *Popular Aviation* thumbtacked to my bedroom wall), fold to the sides of the fuselage when the plane is parked on the deck of a carrier. I gaze up at the great shiny steel propeller. It must be eight feet long. Behind it is the huge radial engine, angled toward the sky as the plane sits there almost all engine, with its single cockpit in the stubby fuselage that drops back to the tiny tailwheel.

While I admire the plane, Mama has started chatting with a man at the edge of the crowd. I recognize him – Ferrin Fraser, who writes the "Little Orphan Annie" radio show from his home at Childs, down where route 98 meets The Ridge Road three miles north of our house.

Here comes Captain Boone. He is strolling across the field from where its far corner meets the Wilcoxes' back yard. Mrs. Wilcox is with him. He is the picture-book flier: reddish blond hair, ruddy complexion, sharp well-trimmed reddish-blond moustache, strong crow's-foot creases at the corners of his eyes, brown leather jacket. Tucked under his arm is a shoebox.

He greets Mama at the edge of the crowd. They've met before. She introduces me. He gestures with the shoebox. Elizabeth made him a lunch. He didn't have time for a sit-down lunch, is putting in his monthly flying time, has to get this buggy back to Washington by four o'clock. But on a day like this he couldn't resist flying up to this part of the world. He steps to the plane. The crowd edges away, widening the circle around the plane. He grasps the edge of the cockpit, puts his right toe into an indented step in the fuselage, swings aboard. Now he is pulling on his leather helmet and adjusting the goggles up on his forehead.

The big propeller moves slowly, as if it doesn't want to turn. Then a sudden cough, a burst of blue smoke between the wheels, a tremendous roar, and the propeller is invisible.

The plane moves. The tail swings around sharply, so the engine is facing the crowd. It revs up. I realize that Captain Boone has set his brakes and is doing his run-up. The roar increases from tremendous to totally deafening. A huge cloud of brown

46

dust is rising behind the plane, billowing into the sky. Through it I see Mama and Ferrin Fraser. Somehow, engrossed in conversation, they have meandered to the wrong side of the field. They are directly behind the plane, in the full blast of the engine, eating its dust.

I wonder what I should do. Run around behind the plane and tell Mama and Mr. Fraser which way to go? How do I know which way? They are standing still. Does Fred Boone know they are there? When he starts to taxi, he won't be able to see anything straight ahead –no pilot can when his tailwheel is on the ground.

The roar dies down. Back to idling. Now Fred Boone guns the engine a little, and the plane starts to move. The tail swings toward Mama and Ferrin Fraser, the nose swings away from them, the plane turns in a tight circle before the crowd and, bumping and wobbling on the rough ground, moves off to the east. Mama and Ferrin Fraser walk back toward the rest of us. They are covered with light brown dust.

I look down the field. The plane is a toy in the distance, far, far down the long field. It is directly in front of the tall woods there, now turning toward us again.

I can see it getting bigger before I hear the roar. Then, suddenly, the great sound bursts at us and in seconds Fred Boone's Grumman zooms over us, maybe 50 feet, maybe 100 feet above our heads. We pivot in unison to watch him climb to the west. Now he is turning south, toward far-off Washington 500 miles away.

But wait. He keeps on turning. He is in a climbing turn, moving up fast, already not much more than a speck. He is almost directly above us. The sound is a quiet purr high in the sky.

And here he comes. A growing roar. Deep. Power. Loud, louder, louder still. The speck is a plane. A biplane. A Grumman. Coming at us. Coming to get us. A power dive right out of a Spencer Tracy movie.

He pulls out when we can read the Navy insignia on the underside of the wings. On his pull-up he heads west again, climbing rapidly, now banking left to head south as he climbs. In moments he is a speck, the sound is a drone. He is gone. I think of him alone up there in the cockpit opening the shoebox, unwrapping the waxed paper, munching his egg salad sandwiches.

E. W. Wilcox Hardware hasn't long to live. Soon after the end of World War II it is gone. Harold Hawks blames its demise on The Town Club, on the third floor up above his drugstore and the bank. "Bud Wilcox spent too many afternoons up there," he says huskily. "My dad taught me to be in the store when it's open and play when it's closed."

# 7

## "You Go Up Like That Yourself?"

McNall and McNall Furniture is next door to E. W. Wilcox Hardware. It has the widest storefront on the west side of Main Street, with a single great plate glass window the width of two stores, and the door set well back into the store at the left corner. McNall's size is matched only by Merrill's Furniture, which is on the east side and almost directly across the street. McNall's has one big advantage over Merrill's: an elevator, one of only two elevators in town. The other is in Arnold Gregory Hospital, up on South Main.

I'm around when the elevator is installed, because Tom McNall and I have been pals since we started school together in primary grade. When we're in the fourth grade, the entire store is remodeled, top to bottom. The elevator is put in to take people and furniture from the main floor up to the second and third floors, or down to the basement. The whole store, Tom tells me, is a new idea –it is all rooms. Instead of a vast sea of furniture in a space the size of the entire floor, like Merrill's, McNall's will show furniture in natural-looking rooms, just like at home.

Tom and I are poking around in the basement the first time the big delivery truck backs down the ramp right into the basement. The place is still a mess. We pick up countless flat round metal slugs, the size of nickels, punched out from the electricians' junction boxes, and wonder what we can do with them. We check out the workrooms, where Tom White, a tall, thin man who is head craftsman in charge of final polishing and delivery, presides. It is only a couple of years later that Tom McNall tells me, in a whisper when he comes back to school from lunch at home one day, that Tom White dropped dead that morning in the shop.

On the grand re-opening day, Tom's big brother, Burt, is the elevator operator. Burt is a year older than my brother Bill, but two years ahead of him in school because he skipped a grade. He gets a load of people aboard on the main floor and tells them, "Face the door, please," so they all turn toward the front of the store and Main Street. At the second floor, he again announces "Face the door, please" with a straight face – then enjoys seeing their confusion as he opens a door at the opposite end of the elevator, facing the rear of the store and away from Main Street. Many of his passengers have never ridden an elevator before. Almost none have been in one that opens at each end. "Saves a lot of fuss and bother when you move out a double bed," says Burt. "No back-and-forthing around the corners."

At Christmas time, I find Burt working in the McNall Gift Shop – another feature introduced in the remodeled store. It is on the main floor, just half way back, a tiny shop with its own door and curtained windows. Inside are candles and candle-holders, bric-a-brac, cookbooks, kitchen towels and potholders, spice racks, coasters, corkscrews, and one gadget after another. "Something for Mom," muses Burt.

50

"Hmmm . . ." Then he darts across the little room. "How about this?" he says. He picks up a flat box that is lying open inside its own top. In it is a shiny thin piece of metal that looks like a giant comb, with 15 or 20 thin tines that are about four inches long. It has a handle at one end that looks like mother-of-pearl.

"What is it?" I ask.

"A cake-breaker," says Burt firmly. "It'll give her great ideas." He grins.

We use it at home for years, long after we're all grown. I see Burt McNall grinning every time.

Tom and I make model airplanes – balsa wood and tissue paper, cut out with a razor blade from thin flat sheets of balsa imprinted with the parts, glued with Duco cement, powered by rubber bands. Our results aren't bad. They fly.

But Burt's are prize winners. He knows how to make the perfect model plane. He tackles ambitious kits – big 24-inch wingspan jobs from The World War, even the Fokker tri-plane – and makes them perfect. Soon the McNall house, up at the corner of South Main Street and East Avenue (the neighborhood where Albion's finest homes stand), is the center of model-airplane activity. Burt stocks kits, opens a store in his bedroom, moves all his clothing out of his closet to make room for his inventory, and does a thriving business.

Burt is relentless. A plane on which he has spent countless hours catches on a tree branch, punching a hole or two in a wing. "That's it," says Burt. "Let's watch this baby go." He takes it up to his bedroom, climbs out onto the broad, gently sloping porch roof, installs a firecracker in the cockpit, winds up the rubber-band engine, holds the plane in one hand by the nose so the prop won't spin yet, lights the firecracker, and launches the plane. It climbs eagerly 20 or 30 feet and explodes.

My proudest moment comes when Burt hangs my silver Luscombe Phantom, along with his Sopwith Camel and one of Tom's planes, in the McNall and McNall show window on Main Street. He hides an electric fan behind a big armchair in the corner, so its blast bounces off the wall and keeps the planes swooping and diving above the living room that's on display. Mr. McNall doesn't seem to mind. The effect is spectacular at night, when the store is closed and the window area is brightly lighted. People on their way up Main Street to the Rialto, or strolling down the street after the movies, pause in wonderment, for you cannot see the fan from out front.

Mr. McNall is a quiet man. I see him at breakfast. When we reach seventh grade, we are in the high school building. That means we move from the Grammar School on West Bank Street to the big new building on East Avenue. I ride my bike the mile from home up North Main Street to The Four Corners, on up South Main another mile to The Avenue, and left on East Avenue another half mile to the high school. But at the corner of South Main and East Avenue is Tom McNall's house. I become his alarm clock. I'm there knocking at the side door – actually, the kitchen door, with its own wide porch facing the driveway loop – before he is out of bed. Mrs. McNall is a tall, buxom woman in a heavy cotton robe. Her hair is pulled straight back, gathered in a tight bun at the top of her neck. She goes to the foot of the back stairs, where they turn above a landing three steps up, and calls, "Tom! Bernard's here!" Then she invites me to have a glass of juice. Mr. McNall is at the dining room table, dressed for business, reading the Rochester *Democrat &*

*Chronicle*. It becomes a daily routine. Tom rumbles down the back stairs, races through the kitchen, finds me sitting with Mr. McNall at the table, grabs a piece of toast, gulps down a glass of orange juice, while his mother says, "Tom, you've got to sit down and have a real breakfast – you can't go all morning on that," and Mr. McNall continues to read the paper.

Mr. McNall wears steel-rimmed glasses. His hair is gray, parted just in the center. His smile lines are deep and friendly. He walks with a limp – left over, Tom tells me, from a boyhood encounter with a wire cable used to slice a haystack in half in the barnyard on his father's farm. I nod knowingly, for I have seen such half haystacks – like giant 20-foot half muffins sliced right down the center, half standing there, half gone who knows where – in barnyards here and there, and I have wondered how that flat vertical face was made. Always after Tom's explanation, when I see a haystack I see Mr. McNall on the haystack, caught by the cable, his leg cut nearly through.

The summer after seventh grade, the McNalls drive west. Tom has talked about it all spring – the Grand Canyon, Pike's Peak, Yosemite. They will see it all. He comes back and announces that Bryce Canyon gets his vote as the most spectacular of all. But the trip has worn out Mr. McNall. He did all the driving, at the wheel of their big Chrysler. And, says Tom, on Mondays and on Tuesday mornings, they burned rubber getting to towns where Mr. McNall could attend the Rotary Club luncheon and keep his attendance record perfect. Exhausted, Mr. McNall looks gray. Within a few months, his heart quits.

Burt graduates from high school at 16 and wins a scholarship at M.I.T. The summer after his freshman year, an M.I.T. crew is manning the launching winch at the annual glider meet at Harris Hill, down near Elmira, New York. It is the third or fourth summer that I have convinced Dad that I absolutely have to spend a day there seeing the soaring planes yanked silently into the updraft off the hill and watching them climb, in their slow, steady, majestic circling, to the underbellies of the fluffy cumulus clouds.

It takes almost all morning to drive to Elmira. We wind our way to the top of the hill, park under some trees at the edge of the field, and meander through a dozen or more sailplanes lying this way and that in no particular order, each flopped over on a left or right wingtip.

I look around, hoping to see Dick du Pont or Chet Decker, two of the top sailplane pilots. They were here last summer, and I've read about them over the winter. I wonder if Peter Reidel, the German flier with the Olympic rings and the swastika on his rudder, has come back. I remember watching him study a map spread out on the tilted wing of his plane before he took off in search of a distance record summer before last.

We can see the launching winch far off across the field. We head toward it. "Where you going?" says a man wearing the gold-braided blue overseas cap of the American Legion.

"Hiya, buddy," says Dad, without breaking stride. "I've got a boy out on the winch."

"Okay," says the Legion man. We move on. It is the first time I've ever heard Dad use that expression. I realize that "Hiya, buddy" is the Legion password.

The winch is parked at the edge of the field, just where it begins to drop abruptly toward the valley. The pitch is so steep you feel as if you could jump off and land 500 feet below. I ask myself how they manage to cut the meadow so well, down over the edge there.

Here's Burt McNall saying hello. He has grown a moustache since I last saw him, and his freckles are darker and bigger. "Feel that breeze off the hill?" he is saying. "If you could stand out there about ten yards, it'd take you right up in the air."

A small bell rings twice somewhere on the rig. "Oops, we've got business," says Burt. "Excuse me."

He turns to the winch. It is mounted on the flat deck of a Ford Model A pickup truck. The truck's rear end faces the field and is up on blocks so the wheels are clear. Part of the truck deck has been cut away above each wheel. The winch has a wheel and tire mounted above each of the truck's rear wheels. Burt grabs a handle just above the winch's drum. "Let 'er run!" he yells.

Now I see there's a man sitting in the cab. He steps on the gas. Burt pushes the handle. The winch's wheels drop down and engage the spinning wheels of the truck. A line of half-inch hemp that has been lying limply in the grass springs up into the air, stretched tautly across the field and starting to move toward the winch. It flies onto the winch's drum through a frame about six inches square. As Burt now takes hold of a small handle on the frame, I see that the square is a miniature guillotine. A knife blade is positioned at an angle at the top, with a strong spring clip ready to snap it downward. Burt turns, gazing downfield.

A gull-wing soaring plane is coming toward us, rising quickly to 20 feet, 30 feet, 50 or 60, maybe 100 feet in the air. We can hear the line sizzling onto the drum as the truck purrs quietly. Burt is squinting at the plane. "Okay," he says to himself, almost under his breath. "Let 'er go! Let 'er go!"

Not yet above us, the plane dips slightly, its nose seeming to nod good-bye, and the taut line suddenly wriggles, becomes a long snake hanging in the air, and in slow motion settles downward as the sailplane soars out over the bluff. I look at Burt. He says, "Okay," and takes his hand off the guillotine trigger. I look up again. As if snatched by an invisible elevator, the plane is growing smaller and smaller, climbing into the bright sky yet scarcely moving forward.

"You go up like that yourself?" Dad asks Burt.

"Sure. When they let me. We don't get too many chances."

Hitler invades Poland. We hear that Burt McNall has quit M.I.T. and enlisted in the Royal Canadian Air Force. He trains as a pilot, flies bombers up from Africa across the Mediterranean, and is shot down.

His mother cannot reconcile herself to Burt's death. She has had a letter from a Canadian who flew for a while in Burt's crew. He tells her they always knew that if there was any way they could get back from trouble, Burt would get them back. When the war ends, she is reading the *Buffalo Evening News* one day. In it is a photograph of a group of 15 or 20 Canadian fliers who have just been released from prison camp in Germany. She is sure the one on the far right, standing at the end of the first row, is Burt. She stops Dad on the street downtown, shows him the clipping. "You see?" she says. "That's Burt. I know it's Burt. You're a lawyer. How can I find him?"

There is, of course, no way she can find him. But I find Burt – his hand ready on the guillotine trigger, his eyes studying the plane aloft – whenever I think of the endless breeze, strong enough to take you right up in the air, that climbs steadily up the face of Harris Hill.

**"Get On Your Feet, You Boys. That's 'Dixie.'"**

Next door to McNall & McNall, on the south side, is one more small shop. Early in my childhood, it is a children's clothing store run by the father of my schoolmate, Amos Beedon. But it closes soon after the day when Amos's big brother, Bill – just turned 16 and permitted to drive on the Junior License that New York State has installed – goes downtown to bring his Dad home for dinner and finds him dead in the back room of the store, killed by his own gun and the Depression he cannot cope with. Amos's mother, Blanche Beedon, is a sister of Bud Wilcox (E.W. Wilcox Hardware). His big brother John is killed in the Navy in World War II. His big sister, Betty, is a tomboy who plays sandlot football with us on the open lot behind the Baptist Church, which is across the street from the Beedons' big house at the corner of Liberty and Park.

The Beedon shop is replaced by the Orleans County Savings and Loan Association. None of us ever goes there, any more than we go to the Gas & Electric store at the north end of the building. But within a few years the Savings and Loan must expand. They buy half of the front yard of the house next door and add a small wing ("a carbuncle," says Dad) to the business building, doubling their sidewalk frontage and creating an L-shaped interior.

The house next door is the first of three residences that still stand side by side on the west side of Main Street in the downtown business section. In fact, they are the only homes in the area of The Four Corners. This one is red brick, classic Greek Revival built probably in the 1830's, with a four-columned portico on the left and a smaller wing, fronted by a side porch, on the right. The way its elegance is spoiled by the carbuncle in the front yard drives Dad crazy. "Nobody in this town ever heard of zoning," he says. "How can they let a thing like this happen?"

Next door to the south is yellow brick. It is the big Victorian house where both Doctor Coopers live and practice medicine. Doctor David Cooper and his wife, Doctor Dorothy Cooper, are Albion fixtures. He has his patients, she has hers, but all occupy the same waiting room, through the door in the wide wing just to the right from the house's big front door.

When I think of the Coopers, I think of the Lattins. Doctor Will Lattin and his wife, Doctor Cora Lattin, practice medicine in their big stone house down on North Main Street, about half way from the canal to the town line and our house just beyond. They are older, much older, than the Coopers, and are pretty much into retirement when I am a very small boy. But Doctor Will Lattin lives well up toward 90 and continues to drive his green 1928 Ford Model A roadster ("one of the first they put out," he says with a grin) until gas rationing stops him in World War II. And when he drops in at our house, walking in stiffly and bent over, he spies the piano, sits right down, and plays *Turkey in the Straw* so our toes start tapping.

Next door to the Coopers, to the south and uphill on Main Street, is another house. Like the other two houses, it is set well back with a broad lawn in front. It is the color of yellow brick, but is stucco covered. I never know who lives there.

South Main is sloping upward now toward Courthouse Square, the high point in Albion topography. Another business building is at the edge of the sidewalk. Its first store is a tiny dairy shop, no more then 10 feet wide and maybe 12 feet deep, just big enough to hold a refrigerator case and two or three customers at a time. The place is nameless and faceless, but it is always there and people go in with empty milk bottles and come out with full ones.

Next is a dress shop. Its paint is a creamy off-white or ivory. Its show windows are set high up, their floor only just below my eye level. Customers going in at the right front corner must climb three steps. Like the little dairy next door, the store is nameless, for no sign hangs overhead. Mama never shops there.

The Rialto Theatre. Here is Albion's movie palace. Its marquee stretches a good 12 feet, maybe 14 feet, out over the sidewalk, and runs the full 20 to 25 feet of the theatre's frontage on Main Street. At each end of the marquee, white light bulbs flick on and off in a never-ending chase around the big lighted rectangle that announces what's showing. The pattern is always the same: A big single feature plays Sunday and Monday nights, a double feature Tuesday, Wednesday, and Thursday, and usually a western on Friday and Saturday. Early show at 7:00, late show at 9:00. Always a Saturday and Sunday matinee. The Saturday afternoon show almost always includes a western serial. Every show includes news and some combination of a cartoon, a Pete Smith Specialty, a John A. Fitzpatrick Travelogue ("and as the sun

60

sinks slowly in the west we take our leave of lovely Pago Pago"), a Robert Benchley short, and previews of coming attractions. Admission is 25 cents at the matinees, 35 cents at night, with those under 12 getting in for a quarter.

Inside, the lobby slopes upward. You walk past the big posters in deep, lighted frames that proclaim the glorious features to come. On the right at the top of the slope is the box office. Mrs. Martina, wife of Rialto owner Charlie Martina, sells the tickets. Charlie bought the Rialto in the mid-'30's from W. H. Robson, who built it and several others like it in Western New York towns and whose will is in the safe in Dad's law office.

Just beyond the box office are four wide doors side by side. Only the right one is open for you to enter the theatre. Charlie Martina, a short, somber-looking man with silver hair, is hovering there, watching you come in. But he does not take the tickets. Johnny Scopa takes the tickets, tearing them in half and dropping one half in the tall box with the slit in the top as he hands you back the other half.

The Rialto probably holds 500 people. The walls are a deep, deep green, almost black. So is the lofty ceiling, except for a large oval maybe 25 feet long in its center. Recessed inside the oval is a painted sky with soft, fluffy cumulus clouds ready to hoist a sailplane upward.

The Rialto is where I see my first movie, a Ken Maynard western at a Saturday matinee. I am shocked at seeing cowboys killed in gunfights, and find myself wondering if they really had to kill people to make movies. I decide they must have faked it some way.

61

The Rialto is the scene of humiliation and embarrassment. It becomes a family habit to get there just in time for the start of the feature in the early show, then see the short subjects when they come on before the start of the late show. But when the Previews of Coming Attractions start, often in the middle of the short subjects (you can tell, because the news has not yet been shown), Mama announces in a voice that can be heard for at least several rows around us, "Well, come on, we're certainly not going to sit through those awful previews." She is on her feet at once, putting on her coat and pulling at me or whoever of my brothers is nearest to her. Dad is not there, if it is a weekday night, for, as a New York State Court of Claims judge, he is usually off somewhere around the state holding court.

"But I want to see them," I protest.

"Then you'll just have to walk home," she declares, pushing off toward the aisle. If it is winter, and quite dark, of course, she is not likely to carry out that threat. But meantime people are straining to see around us.

Far worse is when a movie contains *Dixie*. Mama is from Alabama. The moment the music starts, she is on her feet. "Get up. Get on your feet, you boys. That's *Dixie*." We stand, those behind us leaning this way and that to try and see around us, as long as the music lasts. In certain pictures, it comes and goes any number of times, depending on the period and locale of the story, and up we get each and every time. If Dad is with us, he gets right up, though he's a Yankee native of this town.

In my younger, earlier days of this terrible embarrassment, I seem to hear snickers and I feel eyes drilling into the back of my head. I blush beet red even in the pitch darkness of the theatre. But later I kind of enjoy the performance. It does set us apart. No one else in Albion has a mother who orders her family to their feet to honor *Dixie*. And the interesting thing is that, no matter how many times we stand, no one in the audience ever yells "Down in front!" Not once.

When we come out, if it is the last night of the program, a stepladder is always at one end of the marquee. I look up and see the little man with the big wart by his nose changing the letters on the lighted sign. He is wearing the beat-up brown fedora, with its brim pushed up in front, that never comes off his head. He stands on the tiny platform at the very top of the stepladder, grasping the edge of the marquee with one hand while he stretches to hang the letters on the taut wires across the sign. He is the projectionist. Sometimes I see him look at his watch, step down one step, carefully bend down to grab the top of the stepladder, then scramble down and hurry into the theatre. He knows the reel that is running all by itself is about to end and he'd better get up to the booth to switch projectors.

Johnny Scopa is always standing on the far edge of the sidewalk, his back to the curb, watching people come out. His shiny black hair is sleeked back. If the weather is mild, he is wearing a sleeveless sweater over his white shirt with the cuffs unbuttoned and rolled back one fold. If Dad is not with us, his greeting is, "Hi, Mrs. Ryan. How's the judge?"

Dad goes and comes across the state by train from Rochester, 33 miles away, or from Batavia, 18 miles away. Usually he leaves on Sunday afternoon and returns Thursday or Friday night, depending on the court calendar where he is sitting. When any of us is sick, or for any of a dozen other reasons, Johnny Scopa is called. He drives our car to take Dad to the train or to fetch him home.

Johnny is total calm, total dependability. Nothing fazes him. Mama calls him on a bleak January day. "Johnny, the judge just called from Albany. His case broke up. He'll be coming to Rochester on the Empire. Now, you know the roads are a sheet of ice. What do you think?"

"What time, Mrs. Ryan?" says Johnny.

Johnny is drafted in World War II. While he is in the army, Mama stops by every now and then at his mother's house, out East State Street. "Hello, Mrs. Scopa," she says. "I was over this way, so I just thought I'd stop in and see how you are. What do you hear from Johnny?"

On one such visit, Mrs. Scopa says, "He's-a finished the basic."

"Oh," says Mama. "Then where are they sending him?"

"He's stay there. He's-a the baseball man."

"He's what? Baseball?"

Mrs. Scopa smiles and nods. "He's-a the umpire. They like him there. For the baseball."

It is true. During basic training, some staff sergeant has arbitrarily appointed Johnny Scopa as umpire of a baseball game between two companies. He has been discovered – resolute, decisive, unswervable. He spends the next three years in uniform umpiring one ball game after another until the war ends and he returns to the Rialto and its ticket box.

On another visit, Mrs. Scopa says, "I'm glad-a you came. Wait." She goes into a back room in the little house, returns with a folded thickness of cloth wrapped loosely in brown paper. "For you," she says. "I make-a. For you."

Mama spreads open the paper. The folded cloth is an intricately crocheted tablecloth. "Why, Mrs. Scopa," she says, "you shouldn't have done this."

Mrs. Scopa pats Mama's arm. "I like-a you."

We sit down to Thanksgiving and Christmas dinners on that beautiful lace cloth for 40 years afterward.

The Rialto. We are in and out of that movie house once or twice a week – sometimes three times a week. But never on Sunday. I am 19 years old before I ever see a movie or a play on Sunday. Other entertainment on Sunday, yes. The Sunday night lineup of radio shows – Jack Benny, Fred Allen – yes. But no movies.

Some people at that time take Sunday even more seriously. At home, on a blustery Sunday afternoon in March, my brother Bill and I are flying kites out in the big open field behind our house. We have box kites – newfangled red-white-and-blue kites that fly eagerly, brought home from Albany by Dad. Next door, to the south, the Miles family has rented the Fred Ferris farm. Moved in a couple of months ago. They have three sons, all older than we are. Big, strapping farm boys in their young teens.

Some motion across the field, in the barnyard next door, catches my eye when I am not looking up at my kite. The Miles boys, all three in their denim overalls, have noticed us. They have come out to the edge of the barnyard, maybe 100 yards away, and are leaning on the fence watching us. Suddenly Mr. Miles is there. He shouts at them. I can hear him faintly. "Not something to do on Sunday" reaches my ears as the three of them turn and head across the barnyard, up the steps onto the side porch, and into the farmhouse.

A week or two later, the March wind is even stronger. I launch my box kite on Sunday afternoon, and I fly it until it is getting too dark to see it up there. All my kite string is paid out from the foot-long stick I had wound it on. The ground has thawed enough to be soft underfoot. I jab the stick into the ground at an angle against the steady tug of the string, step back, and look up. In the dusk, I can barely see the kite, but I can hear it rustling and crackling in the west wind.

After dinner, I hurry out in the dark to the edge of the field. I can hear my kite still rustling high above the trees.

It is there when I leave for school on Monday morning. And on Tuesday. And it is still there when I leave for school on Wednesday morning  I hear it even before I look up to see it. Nearing home on Wednesday afternoon, I look above the treetops. No kite. As I come in through the gate at the south driveway, I see its red, white and blue high in the maple tree near the south porch. I hope the Miles boys have watched it on Monday and Tuesday while they did their after-school chores in the barnyard.

# 9

## "The Edge of that Bridge Had to Come Down
## Right Past that Fellow's Nose."

A narrow door beside the theatre lobby leads upstairs. Doctor Dollinger and Doctor Cramer are up there. Dentists. I go to Doctor Cramer once or twice when I am very young, before we switch to Doctor LaLonde in Rochester. Doctor Dollinger leads a parade of Dollingers into church every Sunday: Ann, who is in my grade, Bill, who is two years ahead of us, Peggy, who is even older, Ralphie, who is five years or so younger than I. They all look alike – pale skin and pink cheeks, each face a T of straight eyebrows and straight nose.

Next door toward State Street is another nameless store. Its trim is painted a chocolate brown. In its show window are dusty sections of galvanized stovepipe, an electric motor (like the one Walter Magowan lugs into our cellar when he fixes the pump), a few odds and ends of plumbing supplies. The store always looks dark and dismal. I never see anyone go in or out. A stairway beside this shop has the letters "I.O.O.F." painted on the glass in its door. Upstairs, a bay window projects over the sidewalk. When you step back to the curb, you can see the words "International Order of Odd Fellows" painted on the center window there. In warm weather, when the windows are open, you can hear the crack of billiard balls as you walk by beneath.

Here the sidewalk changes. The cement squares no longer reach to the curb. Now, between sidewalk and curb, there is a width of sod maybe five feet across, and big maple trees – two or three of them – stand in a brief row to the corner of Main and State. On the right as you walk up to State a retaining wall of native stone starts about four feet high and its top level diminishes as the sidewalk slopes up to State. Behind it is the level lawn of The Swan Library, a big red-brick building with heavy Medina sandstone steps that was once an Albion mansion.

I go to the library for the first time when I am in first grade. The place is deadly quiet. The smell is musty. The books line the walls of dark, high-ceilinged rooms. Back toward the rear, where two or three rooms seem to meet, is the check-out desk – a more brightly lighted area. A whispering unsmiling woman tells me to be sure to bring the book back on time, or I will have to pay a fine of a penny a day.

I go through the book right away. Then I put it on a chair in my room. Soon it is buried. I forget the due date. When it comes up for air, the book is a week overdue. Soon it is two weeks. I consider carrying it with me on my walk up Main Street to school and tossing it into the canal as I cross the Main Street bridge. I reconsider. I take it with me to school and on my way home in the afternoon, my heart pounding, I climb the big stone steps into the library and present myself. The librarian says, "Tsk, tsk," as she looks at the due date. The fine is 17 cents. I never take another book out of The Swan Library.

State Street. Here the trolley line comes through town on its way from Rochester to Lockport (or vice versa), running in the center of the street. To the left, just off Main toward Platt, is a switch. For only this one block, the line becomes two tracks, so that trolleys can pass each other. I see them as I walk to and from Central School, where I spend primary through third grade – the trolley stopping just short of the switch, the conductor climbing down, poking a steel rod into a hole in a plate in the ground, prying the switch into position to admit the trolley car onto the south track. Sometimes a waiting car is already on the north track.

The trolley line dies before I am out of Central School. The little flat one-story stone building just behind The Swan Library, which contains the ticket office and waiting room, is remodeled into a home that still stands today. When it is first completed, it has red trim around the windows and red window boxes full of geraniums and petunias. For many years I wish I could have lived in that house.

The trolley tracks are long-lasting. We learn to ride our bikes carefully on State Street. If we're riding parallel to the tracks and must cross over to the other side, we cut across at a sharp angle, for a bike wheel can easily be caught in the crevice between the steel track and the pavement and that means a skin-scraping spill, maybe even a broken bone.

Looking down on the trolley cross-over is the Orleans County Court House. It is a big red-brick square block of a building, three stories tall, topped by a silver dome that rises another two stories to a cupola with its own small silver dome. The Court House is a landmark visible from miles around, for it stands on Albion's highest ground. Its State Street face is fronted by a three-story Greek Revival porch and portico with four stately fluted white columns.

Dad almost never holds court in Albion. The New York State Court of Claims is a specialized court. Its judges hear only cases in which individuals or corporations are suing the state to recover damages that the state otherwise refuses to pay. These can range from a personal injury claim, in which the claimant must prove that the state was negligent, to a major dispute over the cost of construction of a state office building when the state changes specifications after the construction contract has been signed. No jury hears the case. It is decided by the sitting judge – usually later, after the plaintiff's attorney and the state attorney have filed their briefs, but sometimes directly from the bench. The decision must be agreed to by one of the other judges of the court, who reads the brief.

The state is seldom sued in Orleans County, so Dad rarely sits in this courthouse. But once in a great while enough cases are collected to produce a calendar for his court and he spends a day or two in Albion hearing them. One day when I am in fourth or fifth grade he has an Albion calendar and invites me to stop in after school and see what's going on. I pull open the tall, heavy door at the back of the courtroom and slip into a seat near the rear. The courtroom is the entire first two stories of the building, with a balcony over me in the rear half. Dad is in the center of the bench, high above the floor where a railing sets off one third of the room from the spectators' stalls. He is wearing his black judicial robe. The jury box is empty, and only two or three men are at each of the long tables facing Dad. A handful of people are on this side of the railing, watching and listening.

A lawyer is questioning a witness, who seems to be the man who is suing the state. Apparently he was injured at the Main Street bridge over the canal, and he thinks the state, which owns the canal, is to blame. As his lawyer questions him, he tells how the bridge was up to let a tugboat and a string of barges pass through. He stood at the edge of the crosswalk, watching the barges and waiting for the bridge to come down. It is a "lift bridge" that rises flat and level some 20 feet higher than its down position.

I can picture him standing there. Now he tells how the bridge came down. And he continued to follow the moving barges as the last one moved farther and farther west after it came out from under the bridge. And the steel edge of the bridge, meeting the edge of the sidewalk where he stood, chopped off the toes of his right foot as it stuck out over the edge.

I can see it. I'm seeing the string of barges moving steadily toward the sunset. I have seen it countless times. But now as I gaze at the man in the witness chair and at Dad above him on the bench, I am looking down at the same time, down at my feet. I am the man at the edge of the canal. I see my shoe cut open. I see the gushing of blood. It spurts onto the wooden planking of the bridge walkway, red against brown. It floods back onto the concrete where I stand, red against gray. I feel it. A piercing pain, my toes, my foot, my leg all shrieking at once. My field of vision narrows. I am in a tunnel, seeing the courtroom through a hole surrounded by blackness. I am looking through the wrong end of a telescope. The hole at the end gets smaller. Even smaller, so I can see only the head of the witness. Everything is black.

71

Dad calls a recess. He has seen me turn white. He comes down from the bench. He and one of the lawyers tell me to get my head down between my knees. I revive and walk home.

Long afterward, I ask Dad whatever happened in that case. 'Too bad," he says. "That was that fellow's own fault. The edge of that bridge had to come down right past that fellow's nose. An inch or two away. Otherwise it couldn't have clipped his toes. He just wasn't paying attention. And the sign was right there, telling him to stand clear. I had to find for the state. There was no negligence. They upheld me in the Appellate Division."

# 10

## "You Want to Kill Him?"

Coming down from State Street on the east side of Main, the Presbyterian Church is there at the top of the hill. Its steeple is tall and thin, the tallest of any church in town, like a needle pointing straight up at God. The building is dark Medina sandstone, a deep reddish brown, with three doors facing Main Street. High over the center door is a big stained glass window in memory of Marjorie King Reed, wife of lawyer Herb Reed. She died of pneumonia after doctors scraped her lung trying to remove a chicken bone she had choked on and inhaled.

Mr. Hamlin is the minister. Everyone in town knows that Mrs. Hamlin writes his sermons. She also writes a column – all about how to raise your children – in *The Albion Advertiser*.

The first wedding I ever attend is in that church, just after the war, when my schoolmate Jean Anderson marries Bill's best pal Tom Heard. I cut apple blossoms to help decorate the church.

Downhill from the church is a tiny yellow building, one story tall and maybe 15 feet across, with a center door between two small show windows. The business inside is always changing. It is a beauty parlor. Then it is a dairy, competing with the tiny dairy directly across the street at the end of the Rialto Theatre building. Then it becomes a barbershop. Then it is For Rent.

Next is a long gray building, three stores wide. At its uphill end, its own special sidewalk begins, set directly in front of the stores and reaching out about five feet. This walk stays straight and level at the threshold of each store, while the street's sidewalk keeps sliding downhill, so that at the downhill end it takes about five steps to get back down to street level. The effect is great when you are roller-skating down from State Street. You swerve off the street's sidewalk to the right, gliding onto the building's straight and level walk and making no strokes, to see if you can coast all the way to the end. Then you clunk down the steps and wing your way on down Main Street.

The first store in this gray building is Grandma's shop. Here Dad's mother makes hats for the ladies of Albion and the countryside around. Grandma has made hats in this shop since before the turn of the century – since soon after Dad's father died before Dad was born. It is a time when no lady leaves home without a hat, and a time when no factory makes ready-to-wear hats for ladies. Basic felt or straw shapes, yes, but not finished hats. Ribbons and feathers, bows and plumes – Grandma deftly brings them together to create custom-made hats.

I stop in sometimes on the way home from Central School. The shop is long and narrow and rather dark. The inside walls are gray, like the outside. On the left is a long showcase with a curved glass front, with four or five hats inside it. On the right, half way back, is a doorway with a curtain always pulled to the side. Beyond it is

74

Grandma's workroom, with a small work table and a sewing machine. On the table is a small board, about a foot wide by two feet long, on which Grandma presses ribbons. At one end it shows the dark ghost shape where she always rests the flatiron.

On Saturday nights, Grandma stays in the shop late. All the stores are open until 10 o'clock, busy with farmers and farm wives who have come in to town for their weekly shopping. Long after she dies, Dad keeps the key of her shop on his desk. It is six inches long, solid brass. It must weigh a couple of pounds. He loves to tell how Grandma always said that if anyone gave her trouble walking home from her shop on Saturday night she was ready to rap his head with her shop key.

The shops next door in the gray building are empty. They have no For Rent signs in the windows. They just sit there, dark and gloomy. At their downhill end, a wide opening lets cars drive in behind them to Frank Monacelli's garage and a gas station. When I am eight or nine, not long after Grandma dies, her building is torn down. The gas station gains full frontage on Main Street. When Prohibition ends with the repeal of the Eighteenth Amendment, Frank Monacelli closes up his garage and opens a liquor store down on East Bank Street, just a couple of doors from Main. The gas station – the only one fully within the four-block Four Corners area – thrives.

The Monacellis are a big family in town. Frank and his brother Guido, who runs a small grocery store out on East State Street, are natives of Italy. Frank's son Walter is the one who mows our lawn and tells me how to ride a bicycle. Rose and Elsie Monacelli are twins in my grade in school, look-alike identical twins always dressed alike with their black hair cut in bangs. They are cousins of Walter and his brothers Albert, Carl, and Bill.

75

Albert, the oldest, has clerked in Dad's law office, won a scholarship to Notre Dame, gone on to law school. When Dad is sick in bed upstairs with pneumonia and the whole town knows it – when I am 10, long before there is any penicillin, any sulfa, any other wonder drug, when pneumonia is as likely as not to win out over the endurance and resilience of the patient – Albert appears at the front door. "Hello, Albert," says Mama. "What is it?"

"I've got to see the judge."

"Why, Albert, he's sick. He's terribly sick. I thought you knew."

"I know. I've got to see him. It's about a job. I need his opinion."

"Albert, I wouldn't dream of it. It'll be days before you can see him."

"But I need his advice. I don't know whether to take this job."

"Well, Albert, this is one time you'll have to decide for yourself. You're certainly not going near the judge."

Albert goes away. He makes decisions for himself. Twenty years later, he is flying his own airplane to call on clients.

The next day, Father Howard is at the door. He is the young assistant at St. Joseph's Church. He tells Mama, "I've come to give the judge the last rites."

"You're here to do *what*?" says Mama.

"Monsignor Sullivan and I are going up to Buffalo on a retreat," he says, pushing his way into the front hall and toward the stairs. "We'll be gone a couple of days."

Mama backs up against the foot of the stairs, puts one hand on each newel post at the end of the banisters so she's blocking the way. "Not on your life," she says. "You want to kill him?"

"It's just a precaution. When we're on retreat, we won't be available. We couldn't come if you needed us."

"Well, I guess not. I reckon there's a perfectly good priest at the Polish church over there on Brown Street. And another at the church in Holley. That's just eight miles away. And another in Medina. That's twelve miles. And I know the judge. You give him any last rites and he'll give up. Now you go along to your retreat."

When Doctor Brodie stops by, Mama tells him. "Harriet," he says. "Absolutely right. He'd quit."

Next down the east side of Main Street toward Bank is the McMann Hotel. Here a big brown porte-cochere extends from the building clear out to the curb, with double columns mounted on fieldstone pedestals at each corner. But it is really a fake porte-cochere, for there is no longer any opportunity for horses and carriages, or for cars, to drive under it. It is simply there, over the sidewalk.

The big front door is up three or four sandstone steps from the sidewalk, recessed deeply into the building. We never go in there, but I look in through the big windows when I walk past on the way home from school or from Grandma's shop. After Repeal, fresh lettering appears on the window on the downhill side, left of the door: "McMann Grill. Tables for Ladies." Inside, I can see the end of the bar, a bulky dark shape stained almost black. Its brass rail comes toward me from the darkness to the rear, bends round the curved corner of the bar four or five feet from the window, goes across to the wall at the left. A spittoon sits there in the corner. Usually one or two men are standing there. Mostly, if they notice me looking in, they stare. Once in a while one nods or waves. Once, one tips his hat and grins.


Next door to McMann's is a site that has meaning for us. It is where my grandfather had his grocery store. We have a photo of it. "D. B. Ryan." is lettered on a sign high up between the windows of the second and third floors above the store, and on the fringe of the folded awning over the store window, and at the bottom of the window, and on the side of the big box on the one-horse buckboard delivery wagon in front of the store. On the box, the address – 74 Main. – is added. In each case, the lettering includes the period at the end. D. B. Ryan himself is standing on the store's front step, wearing his straw boater. He is in shirtsleeves and vest, his right hand hanging onto the handle of the awning crank as if he has just raised the awning for the photographer (the awnings of the stores on each side are down). Beside him is a younger man also in shirtsleeves and vest but wearing a white apron. A large sign high in the window proclaims, "IVORY SOAP." in letters well over a foot high, with "IT WILL FLOAT." in smaller letters below. Another sign, in fancy, flourishing lettering, says, "S. R. Van Dusen & Co.'s FRUIT FLAVORING EXTRACTS."

On the sidewalk in front of the store are four bushel baskets filled with potatoes or turnips. Behind them on a low rack are a dozen or so large dark round shapes, each nearly a foot in diameter. Are they watermelons? Giant gourds? They have deep dimples where the stems must have been.

I look closely inside the window, and I am perplexed. Chinaware and glassware are on display. Two or three tall, thick vases. Several pitchers that seem to match the vases. Eight dinner plates standing on edge. Cups and saucers, as nearly as I can make out. Among them all, drinking glasses – what Mama always calls tumblers. What is going on? Are all these inedible items in the grocery window related to the faintly visible sign above them that ends with the word "TEA"? Is there some promotion afoot, some redemption of coupons for china and glass, even in 1890? I cannot ask Grandpa, for he died of pneumonia the winter after this picture was taken, long before I was born and even before Dad was born in May of 1891. (My grandfather's pneumonia resulted from his spending too much time checking on the builders in the cold dampness of our big brick house out North Main Street before they got the furnace in.)

Also in the store window, floating about four feet above the display of china and glass, are two oil lamps with glass chimneys. One is at each end of a horizontal bar at the end of a long vertical bar that hangs down from the ceiling. Outside, rising from the curb behind the delivery wagon, is a handsome gaslight.

Seated on the wagon and tautly holding the horse's reins is a boy, also in straw boater. "That's young Joe McGuire," says Dad when we look at the picture. I know Joe McGuire as an old man. He is the one who steps out into the middle of the Ingersoll Street bridge with the STOP sign when the bridge is about to go up because a tugboat has whistled that it is coming along the canal.

Next door to the right in the photo, on the uphill side of "D.B. RYAN.", is McMANN'S BILLIARD PARLOR. Above "D.B. RYAN." on the third floor, two windows are open. In the left one, a man in white shirtsleeves, vest, and apron is looking down at us from the shadows. He seems to be an uninvited intruder in the photo, hanging back from the window just far enough so the daylight gives us his shape and stance but denies us his features.

Is that the same window from which Chauncey DeLuca looks down on Main Street as I walk home from school in late September? Chauncey DeLuca is a harness maker turned shoe-repair man, and he is a baseball fan. During the World Series, he opens his window wide, puts his radio near it, and turns it up full blast so all who go up or down Main Street can hear the game. Usually a small crowd, five or ten or fifteen men, hangs around down below on the sidewalk, sitting on store steps and on the fenders of parked cars.

## 11

## "Spitting Is Unhealthy."

Now we are across the street from McNall & McNall Furniture, and here is Merrill Furniture. The show window is big, like McNall's, with the door at the corner. In the window you do not see a single room, as you do in McNall's, where it is a living room one month, a bedroom the next, a dining room the month after. You see a vast sea of furniture, clear through to the back of the store: beds, dressers, overstuffed easy chairs, dinette sets, sofas, end tables, dining tables and chairs. But when you go upstairs at Christmas time, you find something McNall's does not have: a toy department that spreads across the width of the store, with counters covered with wind-up celluloid animals and tinny little trapeze performers from Japan and with collections of tricycles and bicycles, scooters and carts. Here I shop for Christmas presents for my brothers.

For several weeks before Christmas when he is 13, Bill is at his workbench down cellar making Christmas presents for our younger brothers. Created from his imagination rather than from kits, they are toy trucks and cars. He uses a hand jigsaw

81

to cut plywood into left and right sides, roofs, hoods, back panels, and radiator fronts that he assembles into vehicles each 10 to 15 inches long. But he lacks wheels.

Dad says, "We'll go see Charlie Howard. He can help with this."

Dad knows Charlie Howard will have the answer, for he knows that Charlie himself has made many toys. We find him in the carpentry shop in his big barn. He wears his dark blue overalls, his wire-frame glasses, and a grin that makes us feel right at home on his farm. As Bill describes his project, Charlie listens carefully. Then he turns to his lathe, pulling a covering sheet of denim from it. "Wheels," he says. "Step over here, Bill."

Charlie reaches to a bin that holds odd sticks and even what I guess to be a couple of posts for a porch banister. He seizes one of those, asks Bill to hold one end while he mounts it in the lathe, then says, "Four times four? You're making four of them?"

Bill nods.

"All right. We'll have to stand back a bit." And with that Charlie turns on the lathe and picks up a chisel. In minutes the piece of banister turns into 16 wheels side by side in the lathe. He turns it off, takes the wood to a bandsaw a few feet away, and in a moment wheels begin hopping onto the floor and rolling in all directions.

Charlie not only knows how to make toys. He knows how to make the scenery for any play that our town's amateur thespians decide to stage to raise money for this or that worthwhile cause. And when he isn't building and painting the sets, he is either onstage in a character role or backstage making things work as stage manager. That talent, combined with his portly figure and ready grin, cast him one Christmas season as Santa Claus. And somebody tells somebody in Rochester, our nearest big city, how Charlie turned into a really great Santa.

Next thing you know, there he is in that city's Sibley, Lindsay & Curr department store, playing Santa Claus for line after line of kids day after day through December. Within two or three years, he builds a reputation as a convincing Santa that spreads widely among department-store executives, and in 1937 he opens the Charles W. Howard Santa Claus School in his home. Its intensive three-day course teaches 10 to 15 men in each of several consecutive classes how to dress for the part and play it believably. His students? Mostly CEO's or presidents of major stores across the country. Being bosses, they can appoint themselves as Santas in their stores.

Charlie drills his Santa students in basic child psychology. He makes sure that each pupil develops into a Santa Claus who looks and acts like the foremost first-class resident of the North Pole. He teaches hair styling and cosmetic makeup, with beards fully attached to the face with spirit gum rather than hung from the ears. Every Santa has to own two red suits, one to be worn while the other goes to the cleaner's. Black boots and belts of genuine leather have to be polished every day or, if even slightly soiled, whenever Santa disappears backstage and leaves his sign saying he has gone to feed his reindeer.

Word gets around. Within a few years, Hengerer's in Buffalo, a department store even larger than Rochester's biggest, proudly puts Charlie Howard in charge of the happiness of small-fry who came in with their mommykins to tell Santa Claus what they want for Christmas.

Now Macy's in New York hears about Charlie Howard. They check him out, and 1946 sees Charlie come riding down Broadway atop the elaborate Santa Claus float that climaxes the annual Thanksgiving Day Parade. Then he is ensconced in the store's toy department for nearly four weeks of installing belief in Santa in the eyes and ears of toddlers or reassuring any older would-be skeptics who arrive – a performance on which Charlie thrives at Macy's for several years.

Meantime, along comes another opportunity for Charlie Howard to put his talents to work. Hollywood's Twentieth Century Fox sets out to make a movie called "Miracle on 34th Street" that is destined not only to win three Oscars but to become a Christmas-season staple year after year on television. Who is the knowledgeable technical consultant the producers find to oversee every aspect of the costuming and performance of Edmund Gwenn in the role of Santa Claus? Charlie Howard, of course.

Merrill's Furniture sells radios, while McNall's does not. When I ask for a radio for my birthday, Gus Grinnell brings it down from Merrill's, stands inside our front door explaining it to Mama and me. It is a Crosley tabletop – wooden cabinet a foot high, high-low tone switch, short-wave switch.

"It's amazing," says Gus Grinnell. "Now, my boy in high school – he's in the orchestra, you know. He listens to music on the air, and he says, 'Hear that saxophone?  Hear that trumpet?' I can't tell one from another. To me it's just music. But he can pick it all out."

Mine is the first radio in our house after the Atwater Kent that Dad bought for Grandma so she could hear Amos 'n Andy.  It is on my bedside table. When I get home after school, it brings me Jimmie Allen's Flying Circus, Og Son of Fire, Skippy, Jack Armstrong. At night I hear the Fitch Bandwagon, the Firestone Hour, the Hit Parade. When I stay home sick, I tune in Vic and Sade, Ma Perkins, Our Gal Sunday. Late at night, KDKA Pittsburgh and KMOX St. Louis are right there in my room. When WJZ New York and WEAF New York bring me the big bands from the Glen Island Casino, I can hear the saxophones and the trumpets.

Next door to Merrill's is Trippensee's Grocery. Mr. Trippensee is an old man, tall and thin. Black bow tie and, above his elbows, black sleeve garters on his white shirt, long white apron dropping nearly to the floor, black trousers and shoes, straw boater on his head summer or winter. Wire-frame glasses. Wisps of straight gray hair sticking out around his ears below the flat hat-brim, and a quizzical look as if he is amused to find you in his store. As he listens to your order, he stands rocking backward and forward from heel to toe with his elbows tight against his waist, his hands folded over the strings of his apron where they are tied in a bow in front after doubling round behind him.

The store is big and empty. It has no shelves of canned goods, no big open square boxes of crackers and cookies. It is almost entirely a fruit-and-vegetable store. Long tables hold flats of tomatoes and lettuce, beets and carrots, potatoes and string beans, apples and bananas and oranges and grapefruit. Few of what is not in season, more of what is, but altogether not what you would call an abundance. Usually when we go in there are no other customers, but sometimes one or two are there. Mr. Trippensee is always alone. He seems to have no helpers or clerks.

Maybe it is because the A & P is next door. This is the A & P on the east side of South Main. It competes with the A & P on the west side of North Main, a block away across the Four Corners. We almost never go to the South Main A & P. It has the same big red and yellow "Great Atlantic & Pacific Tea Co." sign, but inside it sometimes has some item that Mama cannot get at the North Main A & P – and that is why we go there.

But then we stop going to any A & P. The South Main store is managed by Mr. Bloom. He takes sick one day in the fall, and is seriously ill. It is about three weeks before he is well enough to go back to work. When he walks into the store, he learns that the A & P has installed a new manager and he is out of a job. He and Mrs. Bloom have always liked the flower business, so they open Bloom's Flower Shop in the living room of their home at the corner of Liberty and West Bank, just across from Coffey Brothers Gulf. At Christmas time, we stop in. The house is crammed with flowers and customers. Mr. and Mrs. Bloom are all hustle and bustle. Mama swears she will never again buy anything at an A & P as long as she lives (and she lives to be nearly 93).

Within a couple of years the Blooms buy a big old house up on South Main Street, beyond the Court House, convert the first floor into a store, pave the front lawn for parking, and establish a business that is still going strong when their grandchildren are grown.


Beside the A & P is a bakery that is another of the town's nameless shops. No sign identifies it. The Sunday morning sweet rolls and sticky buns from here are better than from Wahl's.

Sayers's Menswear is next. This narrow storefront is the Main Street end of a store that has its big windows around the corner on East Bank Street. It cuts through the block, so you can go in from Main and come out on Bank, or vice versa – like E. W. Wilcox Hardware, across the way. Ed Sayers is a jolly man, always smiling, his thinning blond hair atop a chubby pale face with pink cheeks, his gourd-shaped figure in blue shirtsleeves and dark vest (usually unbuttoned) and his belt buckled so tightly he bulges out above and below it.

Right beside the door of Sayers's, a stairway without a door rises. A sign on a riser five steps up warns, "No Loitering." Higher up, on the left wall as you go up, is an aged, weather-beaten sign lettered on a sheet of tin about two feet wide:

# CAUTION

Spitting is unhealthy.
Spit dries. Its germs rise in the air
for others to breathe.
DO NOT SPIT.


I see this sign often, for Dad's law office is up these stairs. But he did not put the sign there.

Beside the stair, and tucked in behind it, is Gus Revelas's Sweetshop. It, too, lacks a sign, but the popcorn machine that Gus rolls out onto the sidewalk or keeps just inside the door tells you, by smell as well as sight, where you are and what the shop is. On the right, behind the stair, is a marble-topped soda fountain, running back to the rear. On the left is the candy counter – a glass topped showcase in which you see tray after tray of light and dark milk chocolates, fudge of every flavor and color, bonbons, and penny candies. Packaged candy bars are stacked at one end: Baby Ruths and Tootsie Rolls and Milky Ways and Butterfingers and Necco Wafers. Beyond the counter and the fountain, back in a darkness where none of us ever dares trespass, are small round soda fountain tables and chairs with their twisted wire legs and backs, just like those in Hawks's drugstore. We never see any customers sitting back there.

Gus Revelas is a little man, maybe five feet tall. His hair is gray and turning white. He wears his necktie tucked into his shirt between the buttons half way down his chest, well above his white apron. When he smiles, his eyes squint.

Sometimes when I go into Gus Revelas's sweetshop to buy a Tootsie Roll or a Baby Ruth, no one is there. I wait. Maybe two minutes. Maybe five. Then I hear rapid, rumbling footsteps in the wall the soda fountain hides behind. I know it is Gus running down from upstairs. He appears, puffing a little, grinning. "Makin' candy," he explains as he ducks behind the counter.

Gus makes candy on the third floor, one flight above Dad's office and back in the Bank Street end of the building. Every once in a while Dad announces, usually over dinner, "Well, *some* excitement today. I guess Gus got preoccupied with customers downstairs. Something boiled over. Or cooked too long. Or something. We had smoke and caramel smell all through the building. They sent a fire truck over, but they never did blow the alarm. I guess it didn't break out into a real fire."

At least once, it is enough of a real fire to drive Dad and everyone else out of the building and to coat everything in his office with soot.

At the corner is Frank's Drug Store. Harold and Enid Frank together run the tiniest drugstore in the world, maybe 12 feet wide by 20 feet deep. It fronts on Main Street with its door set between two narrow show windows. Outside, along Bank Street, it has no windows. The brick wall is painted with a sign the size of the store proclaiming FRANK'S DRUGSTORE. Inside, a narrow aisle to the right takes you past greeting cards and school supplies to cosmetics and shaving creams and to a dead end where tight, narrow steps twist upward to the left (with a NO ADMITTANCE sign on one riser) to Bud Frank's office and stockroom. Or, if you go left, an equally narrow aisle takes you past a counter crammed with displays to the prescription desk at the rear, where a door lets you out onto Bank Street. If other customers are in either aisle, you must nudge past them with an "Excuse me." The ceiling is lower than in other stores, to provide the built-in NO ADMITTANCE space, and any merchandise that is hangable is suspended from the ceiling. Anyone six feet tall must dodge and duck. Anyone six foot six must stoop anywhere in the store. The Franks themselves are little people, wiry and intense. Enid Frank is the only woman in town who dresses in slacks and a matching vest when she works in her store. Bud Frank wears wire-framed glasses and a pencil behind one ear. His light sandy hair is balding at the temples, thin on top. Their store is always busy. They live on Erie Street, and they have kids – a boy and a girl older than I am.

Their store's back door is two steps up from Bank Street. The same two steps, cut from wide blocks of Medina sandstone, are the foot of the second stairway to Dad's office at 4 East Bank Street. When you reach the second floor, you can turn right to the offices of lawyer Fred Thompson, an almost entirely bald and always entirely serious man who is in partnership with his son, "young Fred." Next door to him is Doctor Dugan, a tall, rather elderly medical man whose door is usually open so you can see into his empty waiting room and who is usually down at the foot of the stairs with the fingers of both hands in the lower pockets of his vest, chatting with passersby. Like attorney Ray Fuller over in front of Hawks's drugstore, Dr. Dugan talks away his day. Beyond his waiting room is the Main Street stairway that Gus Revelas rushes up and down when making candy.

If you turn left at the top of the stairs and start down a long hallway, Dad's the first door on the left. His office comprises two rooms. Miss Shortle's desk is dead center, so you are on her left as you enter. Along the wall she faces – the wall that backs up to the stairway – is a row of big legal-size file cabinets. In the corner nearest the door is a small sink with running water. Behind her is a long work table, then more files running to the outside wall. The two windows are tall and narrow, running almost floor to ceiling, with round tops. Between them stands a large Mosler safe.

In the corner by the sink, to the left as you come in, is a flat-top kneehole desk. Above it hangs a matching wall unit with a wide bookshelf over six pigeonholes, with two shallow drawers and another pigeonhole below. The desk and its hanging unit were there when Dad bought Tom Kirby's 35-year-old law office from his estate in 1922, and they stay until Dad has them moved to my bedroom in the big brick house when I am 10 or so. As I write this many decades later, I am sitting at Tom Kirby's desk.

Also just inside the door, on the left above the little sink, a single large door key hangs on a loop of string from a hook. If you must use the "bathroom," you reach under the little sink and find a roll of tissue to take with you and the key to the third floor. There, down the long dark hallway almost to Gus Revelas's kitchen, the key opens what seems to be an office door on the right. You enter a large dark room, larger than Dad's inner and outer rooms combined. Overhead, by the light from the hall, you can make out a hanging light bulb – bare – with a heavy string to pull it on. At the rear, near the two tall dirty windows at the rear of the building, beyond an expanse of sooty floor that crunches underfoot, a toilet awaits you. No wall is anywhere near enough to mount a tissue holder.

Back in Dad's office, on the right just inside the door, is a kerosene stove. Miss Shortle keeps it filled and operating during winter months. It provides the only heat in the office and has only recently (within my memory) replaced the coal-burning pot-bellied stove that required the daily services of Charlie Berry, who

91

lugged full coal scuttles and carried out ashes for most of the offices downtown. He also shoveled snow for most of the stores.

Just past the stove is the door to Dad's inner office. He sits at a large table-like desk, his back to the outer office. "If I sit over there on the other side, people can see whether I'm in as soon as they come through the front door," he says. Behind him is a solid wall of law books in glass-fronted bookcases, the kind whose glass doors rise horizontally and slide back over the row of books. Opposite him is another solid wall of law books. These are open shelves rising to a height of eight feet, dating from the Tom Kirby days. The books nearly all match. They are big, thick volumes the color of Gus Revelas's caramel, but each has a red square with the title and volume number high on its spine and a black square with the publisher's name lower down. They make a far more arresting pattern, lined up in long, slightly sagging rows on the wall of towering open shelves, than the more recent solid dark brown bindings, with their gold lettering, in the glass cases.

Two windows match those in the outer office, and between them is another Mosler safe, even larger than the first. It stands six feet tall. Somewhere inside it is the will of W. H. Robson, builder of Western New York movie theatres.

Dad's phone hangs on the wall behind him, between bookcases. A lighted globe is suspended above the desk, matching the one over Miss Shortle's desk. On his desk are a dictating machine, Dad's letter opener from Clarence A. O'Brien and Hyman Berman, Registered Patent & Trade Mark Attorneys, Adams Building, Washington, D.C., a blue glass bell paperweight three inches high marked New York Telephone, an oddly shaped chunk of raw green glass paperweight (it is on my Tom

92

Kirby desk today), a fountain pen standing in a desktop holder, and a pile of legal papers and pads. Behind him in the opened bookshelf are several lead soldiers that Bill and I have made in the kitchen at home, pouring melted lead into molds and painting them when they have cooled. In the single wide drawer at the center of the desk are rubber stamps and an ink pad, pencils and pens and scissors. Two of the stamps are my favorites. One says FOUND, the other NOT FOUND. When Dad reads the briefs in cases he is deciding, he stamps the margins and jots his initials if he agrees (FOUND) or disagrees (NOT FOUND) with the legal citations or points made.

Miss Marguerite J. Shortle is a New York State Civil Service employee, transferred to Dad's office in Albion from the Court of Claims headquarters in the capitol building in Albany. She is a squat woman probably in her mid-thirties when she comes to 4 East Bank Street, and she stays some 25 years until Dad retires. She has dimples and wears pale pink lipstick, but otherwise is what I guess you would call plain: brown hair kept short, a tiny button nose, round cheeks, and almost a double chin. She always knows what my brothers and I are up to, where we are in school, where we're going next, our model planes, our skating and skiing, our friends. She gives us Christmas presents – books to match our current interests, imprinted stationery just when we are old enough to relish having our own letterheads. We find Christmas presents for her, too – scarves, gloves, tablemats and napkins for her little apartment – but she is never invited for Christmas dinner. "Once we start that," says Mama, "we can never stop. I just think it's better not to."

Miss Shortle gets out Dad's opinions. He dictates them into his machine, often on Saturdays and Sundays if has been holding court around the state during the week – or on weekdays if he is between calendar calls in Buffalo, Rochester, Syracuse, Utica, Binghamton, Albany, New York, or the smaller county courthouses. Miss Shortle handles the constant flow of large flat manilla envelopes containing legal briefs moving to and from the other judges on the court. When Dad is away, she makes at least two trips a day to the smart new red-brick Post Office, up on the west side of Main Street at the top of the hill, at the corner of Main and State and across Main from Court House Square.

If Dad is in town, he likes to make the trip himself. The morning mail is sorted by 10 o'clock, the afternoon mail by 4. Winters, he's in his long gray herringbone overcoat and fedora with the brim turned up in front – summers, his light Palm Beach suit and straw boater. He enjoys those Post Office walks. He always finds someone he knows to chat with – most often Ray Fuller, who is ready to discuss some client's problems.

On one summer day Dad loves to tell about – a balmy afternoon soon after the new P.O. is finished in '36, a sunny afternoon when the white fluffy clouds are breezing along over Western New York – Dad gets up to the top of Main, just in front of the Presbyterian Church, and he can see there's some commotion over in front of the P.O. One fire truck is stopped there. And a wrecking truck from Jimmie Hubbell's Texaco. And the police motorcycle (there is only one in town, a side-car job usually driven by Chief Horace Kelsey unless both cops are going somewhere, in which case the chief rides in the sidecar and Officer Coffey drives).

94

Dad crosses the street. Getting nearer, he sees a small knot of people gathered at the steps of the P.O. The building has only about six steps. They are granite, maybe 15 feet across at the bottom, narrowing at the top to the six-foot width of the double doors – just like a thousand Post Offices built in the '30's and still the backbone of the Postal Service today. At each end, a black wrought-iron railing curves gently down as the steps widen. On the bottom step, each railing winds up in a circle of banisters about a foot in diameter.

And right there is the center of attention. Dad leans in over the crowd (he's tall, which helps his lawyer's inclination to see to the center of things), looking past Police Chief Kelsey and Fire Chief Wally Eggleston and several women and discovering a small boy, maybe four years old. He's the center of attention for an obvious reason: His head is on one side of two of the upright wrought-iron banisters and is inside the foot-wide circle, while his body is outside. His face is streaked with tears.

A young woman who is patting the boy's shoulder sees Dad and says, "I only left him for a minute. Just to buy some stamps. I don't know how he ever got his head through there. And so fast." She has wiped some tears of her own.

Dad watches. The boy's mother and Chief Kelsey, almost together, say, "All right, Freddie. Let's try again." And the Chief takes Freddie's head between his hands and, gently but surely, tries to hold it at an angle so it will come back out from between the iron bars, while Freddie's mother guides his shoulders. Freddie winces, then starts sobbing.

95

They quit. "No use," said Chief Kelsey. "Wally, you better set up the torch and cut this thing up."

"Nope," says the Fire Chief. "Couldn't keep the sparks off the boy."

"I'll hook a chain up and pull a bend into one of those rods," says Howard Dutton, who is working summers at Jimmie Hubbell's Texaco.

"What if it snaps and hits the boy?" says Chief Kelsey.

"Tell you what," says Dad. "I think we've all forgotten the most important thing. How old are you, son?"

The boy turns his head and looks up over his shoulder and through the bars of wrought iron at Dad. "F-f-four," he sobs.

"Well, when we're four years old," says Dad, "our head is the largest part of us. Freddie, you didn't put your head through there. You were around on the other side. You stepped through those bars, didn't you? C'mon, mother. You pick him up by the waist." And Dad goes around behind the rail and takes Freddie's shoulders as his mother picks up his weight, passes his body between the banisters, and Dad sets him down on his feet.

Freddie runs around the banisters to his mom. Chief Kelsey straddles his motorcycle, stands up high and jumps down on the starter. Chief Eggleston climbs up into the fire engine. Howard Dutton hurries off to the wrecker. Freddie and his mother walk away hand in hand in the breezy sunshine. Dad goes in to see what's in box 25.

## 12

### "You Think You Seen Hailstones?"

Beyond the Sayers haberdashery is the Five and Ten. Officially, it is the J. J. Newberry 5-cent, 10-cent, and 25-cent Store, but we never call it anything but the Five and Ten. The man who runs it (for years, until I am old enough to know about chain stores, I think he is Mr. Newberry) wears a dark blue plaid suit and a blue shirt and dark blue tie. His curly black hair is thinning above his permanently creased, worried forehead.

The store is big. Outside, a show window, a double door, a long show window, another double door, another show window, with doors and trim all in bright red paint. Inside the first door, a popcorn machine and counters of candy. Then dry goods: bolts of cloth, broad open display tables of scissors, needles, thread, ribbon. Toward the center of the store, ready-to-wear: ladies' first, with tables of sweaters and blouses and slips and stockings and unmentionables. Men's next: work shirts of khaki and denim, dress shirts, undershirts and socks and underpants and longjohns.

Everything neatly folded on broad flat table-height counters. Nothing above waist level, so you can see all around the store from wherever you stand.

Beyond, on the aisles near the east door, pots and pans, baking dishes, china and glassware, white enamel double boilers – with black rims and handles and black lids, tumblers decorated with red cherries and their green leaves just below their rims.

I buy none of all this. But I must walk through it all to get to the rear of the store, back the full depth of the store and into a smaller, narrower section. Here are the electrical parts – sockets, plugs, rolls of wire, and the carpenter's tools and needs, from boxes of flat-head and round-head screws of all lengths to tiny brads and finishing nails. But best of all, here is the toy and hobby department. Here I get the Duco cement, the single-edge razor blades, the banana oil, the white tissue paper, the extra blocks of raw balsa wood to go with the airplane kits that Burt McNall sells. And here are kits themselves, too.

The Tootsietoy selection is big. It includes most of the cars on the road and many of the trucks. You can buy unfinished raw metal castings of the tiny cars, with little bottles of fast-drying paint – red, blue, green, white, yellow, brown, black – a nickel apiece or six for a quarter.

When I think of Tootsietoys, I think of Roy Rutledge. Roy is in Bill's grade in school. He is curly-haired, eager, always smiling, always enthusiastic. He lives with his grandfather (the only man in town who wears a beard, a scraggly gray beard down onto his chest) in a house set far back behind other houses on Linwood Avenue, an unpaved street off Ingersoll, back two blocks from Main Street and beyond Erie, just on the edge of the Village of Albion's official town line. Roy's house is unpainted, a small, vertical building of no architectural period, with a high- pitched tin roof. His grandfather's Model T Ford sits in the yard. I'm walking home from school one day with Richard Gminski, who lives more or less across Linwood from Roy, and Roy has overtaken us as we near Linwood. It is just after Christmas. We are talking about what we got for Christmas, and in fact I'm going to Richard's to see his presents. Roy invites us to come see his.

We go in through the kitchen, by a side door near the Model T. His grandfather is just pouring a cup of coffee from a big enameled percolator like they have at the chuck-wagon campfires in the western movies. The front room is almost bare. No rug. A plain square table in the center, with four or five straight chairs around it. A small thin evergreen stands near the window, mounted on a single flat piece of board. It wears no Christmas decoration. On the floor under it, a couple of small cardboard boxes. And a Tootsietoy car.

Roy picks up the Tootsietoy, holds it for us to see, puts it on the table and pushes it back and forth. Its wheels are white rubber, its body dark green. He lets us zoom it around the tabletop. It rolls wonderfully on the smooth wood. I remember for a long, long time how pleased Roy is with his one Christmas present and with sharing its fun with Richard and me.

Vince Calloway's Barbershop. Vince is a white-haired, red-faced, roundish man in a white jacket who presides over an entire wall of shaving mugs. Each has its own square box in the shelving, and each has its owner. Here, when I am very small, I first see a barber tilt a man back almost horizontally, then snatch a steaming hot towel

99

from the shiny chrome heater in the corner and wind it round his customer's face to a coiled point over his nose. With wonder I watch the steam rise, hoping Vince Calloway will not do this to my Dad or to me. But Dad and I get only haircuts.

Meland's IGA Market is the only store downtown that has sawdust and wood shavings on the floor, like Palmer's Fish Market in Rochester, where we stop to get whitefish (Bill's favorite dinner) when we are in the city. Meland's is another wide store, with lengthy windows on the outside of which the day's specials are hand-lettered in a thick white paint that never dries – it wipes off when the message must be changed. The trick at Meland's is to stick one finger against the glass and run the length of the window, creating a line that breaks through the lettering all the way across and, as the paint gathers before your sliding finger, makes a thin white smear – without getting caught. I never get caught, because I never quite get up the nerve to try running Meland's window, but Howard Dutton shows us how. He gets a running start from the other side of Calloway's Barbershop, flies past Meland's creating a slightly wavy line through the lettering, and is out of sight around the corner at Platt Street before anyone in the store even notices.

Someone challenges Howard to make a two-fingered double line. Maybe even four? "Nah," he says, his freckled face grinning, "that's too messy. You just want one nice line." And he waits for the signs to change next week.

Maybe he doesn't want to be too messy – or get caught – because the Melands and the Duttons are next-door neighbors on North Main Street, down from the canal almost to Erie Street. The Meland house is big, with a broad porch all the way across the front and a huge single window centered upstairs in the white clapboard wall over the porch roof. Next door, on the right, the Duttons' is a small gray one-story house with white trim, set far back and with a long cement walk going in from the sidewalk. Here, on a Saturday morning when I am in the second grade, I have ridden my tricycle from home to play at Howard's. We have been back and forth around the neighborhood on scooters and tricycles, and I am speeding in toward the Dutton house when I see the front wheel of my tricycle moving ahead of me, rolling speedily by itself on the strip of white concrete as I dive headfirst over the handlebars.

I wake up in the Duttons' kitchen. I am sitting on Mrs. Dutton's lap. She has a cold cloth on my nose. She refolds it and I see that the cloth is bloody. In a few minutes, when I tell her I feel O.K., I walk the half mile home, carrying the tricycle's big front wheel in one hand, the rest of it in the other. Mama is furious. "My fathers! You mean that woman let you walk home all by yourself after all that?"

On Monday, when I walk into my schoolroom with a heavy red scab the length of my nose, everyone laughs. Miss de la Verne shushes them.


Next door to Meland's is Thompson's Newsstand. Newspapers and magazines are piled on racks and shelves on left and right inside the front door. You pay for them at a glass showcase filled with candy bars, cigarettes, tobacco, lighters, and tobacco pouches. Overhead hang cards of corncob pipes and pipes in a dozen shapes. A lunch counter runs back toward the rear of the store.

Thompson's is the Greyhound bus stop, so it is open late at night and all day Sunday. Often after Sunday dinner, I am the one who jumps on his bike (I have a basket on my bike; Bill has none on his) and speed down to Thompson's to get ice cream for dessert. Ice cream is 25 cents a pint, 40 cents a quart and home freezers haven't been thought of yet. I like the trip through the lazy early afternoon of a Sunday, the deserted streets of The Four Corners. Sometimes not a single car is parked downtown except for one or two right at Thompson's. If the Western New York breeze is gusting, which it usually is, small cyclones of dust whirl up now and then, maybe three or four feet in diameter and ten or more feet high. They spin along near the curb, coming east from West Bank Street, and, if conditions are right and you are lucky enough to come along just then, turn the corner and head up South Main. They can't do that when cars are parked everywhere.

There are Sundays when I can ride from our house to the foot of the Main Street bridge and, instead of pumping up the slope to the bridge and the start of The Four Corners, turn left along Caroline Street, reach Ingersoll, turn right and go over the canal on the Ingersoll Street bridge, then right again on East Bank and so to Thompson's – all without passing a single automobile or another biker. Or I can go straight up Main, over the bridge, and left on East Bank to Thompson's, then ride on home by way of the Ingersoll Street bridge, Caroline, and back to Main and home. Either way, on such days, the town is quietly mine.

But one Sunday I am riding down Ingersoll from the bridge, on the way home from Thompson's with the quart of ice cream in a bag in my bike basket, and there is my classmate Arnold Garrison on his bike. He lives on Caroline, just west of Ingersoll. His dad is a barber – Shorty Garrison – with a shop over the Five and Ten. They are a musical family. Arnold's big brother plays the saxophone and, already out of high school, is on tour with a swing band. Arnold brought down the house singing

"Annie Doesn't Live Here Anymore" in his high boy soprano in the American Legion minstrel show that opened the new high school's auditorium last year.

Arnold hails me and we stop. "Where you going?" he asks.

I tell him I'm on the way home with some ice cream.

"Gee," he says, "you have ice cream at your house every Sunday, don't you?"

Not always, I tell him. But we just about do.

Thompson's isn't the same after Mr. Thompson dies. He gets a sore in his mouth. Maybe it's an impacted tooth. Something is open and bleeding. A nurse at the hospital puts iodine on the raw sore. You can't do that. It goes right into your bloodstream or somewhere. Your saliva multiplies the strength of the iodine. That's how they explain Mr. Thompson's sudden death.


The Orleans Hotel stands at the corner of East Bank and Platt. It is like the McMann Hotel on Main Street: a dark brown leftover from the turn of the century. Inside is a big empty lobby area, with a dining room to the rear. We go there once for Sunday dinner, and the room is nearly empty. The tablecloths are stark white silent ghosts. We never go again.


Now we are at the eastern end of The Four Corners. Platt Street heads uphill to the right. Miss Shortle's little apartment is just around the corner, in the first house up Platt behind the Orleans Hotel. Across the street from her is *The Albion Advertiser* office and printing plant, run by Jennie King, who came to town as a young printer's devil before the turn of the century, started the paper as an advertising giveaway years ago, and wears a wig that is an absolute bird's nest sitting squarely on top of her head. The plant is a long stretch of concrete building blocks one story high, running deep on a narrow lot. Somewhere back inside it are Jennie King's living quarters.

Next door, at the southeast corner of Platt and East Bank, is Jimmie Hubbell's Texaco. Jimmie started at Coffey Brothers Gulf, over at West Bank and Liberty, pumping gas and fixing flats when he was in high school. He is one of those guys who was born to fix cars and make people feel good. There is nothing he does not know about automobiles and there is no one he doesn't make a friend. Later, after World War II, he gets the Esso franchise up on East Avenue opposite the high school, where he has a garage three times bigger, with four or five service bays, much more room to park cars waiting for service, and a lot more traffic going by.

I'm at Jimmie Hubbell's Texaco one afternoon putting air in my bike tires. It has been a day of summer thunder squalls and downpours, then sunshine, then more storm. A pickup truck pulls in and stops over near me and the air pump, away from the gas pumps. So it didn't come in to get gas. A farmer jumps out. "Hey, Jimmie! Look at this!"

From the cab, he takes a big thermos jug – the fat round kind with a wide opening at the top and a spigot down front. Jimmie Hubbell comes over. A small crowd gathers. "You think you seen hailstones?" he says. "Look at this."

He takes the top off the thermos. He lifts out a perfectly round chunk of ice the size of a golf ball. Then another as big as a baseball. Two or three that size. A dozen golf balls. He passes them around. "Crop's gone," he says. "Flat. Not one stalk standing. Far as I can see. Three fields of onions. Gone."

He is from the muckland – rich black loam reclaimed from swampland up south of Barre Center on Route 98 nearly to the town of Elba, which is The Onion Capital of Western New York. He pulls off his cap, holding it by the peak as he rubs the back of his head. His forehead is white, but the rest of his face, his ears, his neck are deeply tanned from endless sunny days on the tractor. He needs a shave and his dark tanned hands are big and rough. The fine dirt of the muck is black under every fingernail. I look back at his face and the deep rough crow's feet at the corners of his eyes. Still holding his cap by the peak, he rubs the corner of his right eye with the back of his hand. I realize he is wiping tears.

# 13

## "I Was Thinking of Digging a Trench."

On the north corner of East Bank Street, catty corner from Jimmie Hubbell's Texaco, is the fire house. It is a big red-brick building with a Victorian tower at the corner. The fire whistle is in the tower, and if you are downtown at noon when it gives two blasts – or any time when a fire occurs – you know it. It knocks you off your feet. Two big wooden garage doors painted beige face Bank Street, always open in the summer so you can see the fire engines, headed out and ready, and always closed up tight in the winter. Around the corner, facing the short extension of Platt Street that runs down about 200 feet to the canal bank, are three more fire-engine bays. In the front corner facing Platt is the office. On the Bank Street side outside the office wall is a long bench. Fire Chief Wally Eggleston sits there if things are quiet, waiting to hear the phone ring and chatting with whoever comes along and has time for a word or two.

When the fire whistle blows, it is heard all over town, for its purpose is to call the volunteers. In our phone book is a code of 15 or 20 numbers. Each identifies a location in town. If the whistle blows three times, pauses, then blows five times, you look up 35 and see what part of town the fire is in. If you are a volunteer fireman, you jump into your car and head there – unless you work down at The Four Corners and currently have driver or truck duty. In that case you dash for the firehouse and jump aboard or take the wheel of a truck assigned to you. Sometimes I am downtown when I hear the whistle. I see men running out of stores, racing to the corner, and leaping onto the running board of a fire truck as it roars by.

When the whistle blows a five, the fire is out of town. You pick up your phone, and when the operator says, "Number, please," you ask where the fire is. She tells you, and you head there. You don't have to be a fireman. She tells anybody. And anybody goes.

When you hear just two blasts, you know the fire is out. And in all cases, the code number is blown several times over.

One time, the operator says, "It's in Barre Center. Dale's plant."

I beg Mama to take us. "All right. It's probably a wild goose chase, but we'll go."

Wally Dale's canning factory is the biggest building in Barre Center, about six miles south of town on Route 98. We can see the smoke when we're half way there. Thick black smoke billowing upward, rolling and tumbling eastward with the strong west wind. Traffic is heavy rushing toward it. We park on the edge of 98 and hike past a scramble of cars parked this way and that, through the center, and out to the right on the west road about 800 feet.

We can smell the smoke. Thick. Heavy. We are walking through it as we head west. The wind is bringing it to us. Something about it reminds me of September.

Getting nearer, seeing the smoke rising beyond the rooftops and trees along the west road, I hear a steady hum of engines. Now I see fire engines. They are not only from Albion but from Elba, from Batavia, from Medina. Hoses are like giant spaghetti all over the ground. The hum of the engines is punctuated by soft BOOMs. They have no particular rhythm – just BOOM every now and then, as if someone is beating a bass drum but not keeping time.

Now we see the building. Already the roof is gone and the roaring flames have been cut down. Here and there bright fires lick at the base of the walls. Another sudden soft BOOM – not too loud, sort of mushy sounding, as if it didn't really mean it – and I see a round black object fly up from the building, arch 60 or 70 feet in the air, and drop into the field beyond the factory. Then I look around. Everywhere are black objects. They are lying in the road, among the spaghetti hoses, in the ditch and field beyond the scramble of cars and fire trucks. Another BOOM. I look back at Dale's Canning Plant. Two more black objects rocket up, lose speed, arch over the billowing smoke. One drops out of sight through the smoke, the other comes more or less my way.

I turn back to the round black things lying among the hoses near me. What are they? They are big tomato cans. Wally Dale cans tomatoes in the number 10 can, as big as your head, that is bought by restaurants and hotels and hospitals. In the intense heat, they have exploded, shooting themselves off like cannon fire. "For a while there, I was thinking of digging a trench," says a man in fire helmet, slicker, and boots. He grins and shakes his head.

Then I recognize the odor in the smoke. It is the ketchup smell that hangs over Albion in September when, from sunup to sundown, the Snider plant has farmers' truckloads – and wagonloads – of tomatoes lined up the length of East Avenue back to Main Street (at least a quarter of a mile) and an equal distance up and down Main and is squashing and cooking tomatoes 24 hours a day.

Once, we come as close as you can to a real fire at home. It is 5:45 in the morning, and it is the morning of Christmas Eve. Dad gets up (it is his usual get-up time) and goes down to the kitchen. Its door is closed. The doorknob is warm. He pulls the door open and is hit by a blast of hot air.

The kitchen is attached to the back of the house – literally attached, for it was an afterthought when the house had already been built and Grandma and D. B. Ryan decided to change the floor plan. The wall between the kitchen and the rest of the house is double brick with an air space, altogether about a foot thick. The coal-burning furnace that heats the house has no hot-air ducts to the kitchen, so a big pot-bellied stove about five feet high stands in the far corner, beside the back door, to provide heat when the cooking stove does not provide enough. In December that is most of the time.

Dad realizes the pot-bellied stove is dangerously overheated. It looks a little orange at the base, above its legs. He grabs a potholder and turns the damper in the stovepipe to vent the heat. He turns on the faucet in the sink, fills the dishpan, splashes the walls, creates steam. He opens the back door and the windows. He runs back to his study, just beyond the pantry and close to the kitchen door, and grabs the phone.

109

Wally Eggleston answers at the firehouse. "Wally," says Dad. "You got anybody with you? Anybody who could come down here with a tank of chemicals?"

"Not at this hour. Just me. I'm here alone."

"Don't blast an alarm. I'll call you back if I need you."

Dad goes back to the dishpan. The heat in the kitchen is down. He splashes the wall behind the stove again, to be sure. He mops. He thinks about the big closet in the back room upstairs over the kitchen. In it is everything that Santa Claus expects to bring to our house that night.

**14**

**"Did You Win?"**

Next door to the fire house, on the north side of East Bank Street, is the *Orleans Republican.* Jim Lonergan is the editor, and Mrs. Lonergan runs the paper with him. The paper is a storefront operation, with three or four desks up front near the windows, then a railing and gate like the altar rail in church, then the big printing press, a smaller press, the linotype, and work tables for the men who get out the weekly. The Lonergans and a couple of other people are at the desks, pounding typewriters, taking orders for job printing, talking on the phones.

The paper is big on "Personals" – columns of brief notes on who went calling on whom last Sunday afternoon, who is out of town on a fishing trip, which hospital-benefiting "Twig" had its meeting at whose home last Thursday evening and what the members knitted or sewed or discussed. Mama has a running contest with Mrs. Lonergan, trying to keep us out of the Personals, to the point where Mrs. Lonergan calls Mama, when she hears that we went anywhere or had a few folks in for dinner, before she prints anything. Usually Mama says, "Oh, Mrs. Lonergan, that's not really *news*. Please don't put that in the paper."

In the paper's store window, for a few weeks, is a pedal-powered Model A Ford roadster – a perfect miniature of the big car, sized for a six- or seven-year-old. It is green, like most Model A's, with battery-powered headlights and horn, chrome-plated bumpers, wire spoke wheels, everything. Jim Lonergan shows Dad how the roof folds up and down as I watch eagerly. The car is part of a promotion. It is raffled off. I fail to win it. I dream of that car, and myself at the wheel, for years afterward.

Albion's third A & P is next door to the *Orleans Republican*. Like the others, it is painted bright red, with the big sign over the awning across the top of the store. Mama goes to this one more than the other two (until The Great Atlantic and Pacific Tea Company fires Mr. Bloom from the South Main store for getting sick) and I am glad she does, for this one gives lollipops.

Beside the A & P is the telephone company. It occupies two full store widths, painted a dark green olive color like the mailboxes at street corners. The entry of the first is permanently blocked by a board across double glass doors. The three or four steps needed to reach the doors have been removed. You can look in and see the operators sitting at the big switchboard. In hot weather, the double glass doors are open and screen doors are behind the barrier board. I try to walk by very slowly in the summer, but I can never quite make out what the operators are saying.

The second double doors have their steps. People go in and out to pay their phone bills. Miss Shortle stops to pick up Jody Van Stone, the chief operator, when they are getting together to go to dinner. They have been good friends ever since Miss

112

Shortle arrived in Dad's office. Considering the number of phone calls Dad and Miss Shortle make to Albany and to the other judges' offices around the state, it is not surprising that they got acquainted.

Kudner's stands beside the phone company. It sells ladies' dresses. Its front is different – the only store in town that has been remodeled with panels of shiny black material (is it glass?) that reflects your image as you walk by. I have no idea what Kudner's is like inside, for I never go in there. Mama never shops there. She buys dresses and hats from Sibley's or McCurdy's department stores in Rochester, Hengerer's in Buffalo, or from B. Altman's catalog or its ads in *The New York Times*.

We get the *Times* every day at Kellogg & McCabe's Newsroom, next door to Kudner's. If Dad is not holding court out of town, he brings the paper home at lunchtime. If he is away, Mama picks it up or one of us gets it on the way home from school. It costs a nickel. As far back as I can remember, the *Times* is as important to us, and as regular a part of daily living, as eating. Dad especially admires columnist Arthur Krock, who almost daily hits the nail on the head about whatever is going on in Washington. Dad frequently writes him to tell him so.

Kellogg & McCabe's stands behind a dingy, dark green facade. Its windows need cleaning. On display behind them is a dusty collection of pipes, cigar boxes, lighters, tobacco tins, work gloves, flashlights, key rings and key cases. Inside on the right are counter-height tables on which current magazines are stacked. Two copies of *The New Yorker* arrive each week. We always buy one, for 20 cents. On the left, running back to the rear, is the counter where either Kellogg or McCabe takes the money for the paper or magazine. In the rear, where it is dark and smoky, are three or four or five men smoking cigars and pipes and talking quietly. Sometimes one or two of them nod or wave or smile. Sometimes they are so involved they don't even look up. They always give me a creepy feeling.

Frank Monacelli's liquor store. Its trim is butterscotch-colored. It opens almost the day after the Repeal of the 18th Amendment. (Before then, a quiet lunchroom was there. It seldom looked very busy.) It quickly becomes *the* downtown liquor store, and is an excellent source of sturdy cardboard cartons when we must pack books.

A narrow alley separates Frank Monacelli's from the Bank Street end of Freeman's Drug Store. Like E. W. Wilcox Hardware and Sayers's Menswear on other corners, Freeman's is L-shaped around the store at the corner. It fronts on Main, but the prescription counter is here at the Bank Street end, so you go in here if you know that and are getting a prescription filled. Mr. Freeman is a little man with very little thin gray hair left on top, moustache speckled gray and reddish brown, white shirt and black bow tie, sleeve garters, open vest. Mrs. Freeman's gray hair is twisted in a big knot on top of her head. She sticks a pencil through the topknot when she isn't using it. She wears a flowered smock over her white blouse and tweed woolen skirt. She is even smaller than Mr. Freeman. Her wrinkled face is in a permanent smile. His is permanently dour.

Upstairs are law offices. Ramsdale and Church is the office where Dad went to work at 17 for 50 cents a week back in 1908, running errands to the post office and the County Surrogate's office on Court House Square, keeping the coal scuttle filled and the pot-bellied stove hot, and "reading law" when he could in between. Sanford

114

Church is Grandma's age, married to her cousin Florence Beach Church. They live in Albion's largest Greek Revival home, up on Ingersoll Street at the corner of East State, with a cast-iron fence along the sidewalk at the foot of the great lawn and an official blue and gold cast-iron roadside marker on a tall post. Put up by the State of New York, it notes that this was the home of Judge Church's grandfather when he was Lt. Governor of the state. When we stop in to visit on Sunday afternoons, Judge Church likes to find pennies in my ears. He lets me keep them. But he decides how many he will find.

When Cousin Florence and Judge Church die, Roy Merrill buys their big house and turns it into a funeral home. Soon he closes up his furniture store on South Main and, with Gus Grinnell, concentrates on the undertaking business.

The corner store is Tibbett's Jewelry. It fronts on Main Street and, like Frank's Drug Store opposite, proclaims its presence with a wall-sized sign – white letters on dark green – painted on the bricks facing Bank Street.

Looking back eastward along Bank Street from the corner of Main, I see it on a summer night when the American Legion Carnival is in full play. For a week, barricades keep traffic out of the block from Main to Platt. The merry-go-round is at the Main Street end, the Ferris Wheel at Platt in front of the firehouse. In between are baseball throws, high-strikers, number wheels (you put a penny, nickel, or dime on a numbered square on the counter and get another penny, nickel, or dime if the wheel stops at your number – double if the number on the wheel is red, not black), the Bingo tent, car rides for little kids. In the middle of the block is a bandstand where the

Legion band plays Souza marches at eight o'clock each night. The band is a big group – 18 or 20 members, plenty of trumpets and trombones, several drummers, even a glockenspiel, all in blue uniforms and blue-with-gold-braid overseas caps. They create a glorious peppy sound that brings people back night after night.

My brother Bill cannot lose at Bingo. In one evening, he wins a blue glass salad bowl with fluted sides and a lamp with sailboats on its shade and red and green lights in its brass base, like the running lights on boats. He gives them to Mama. Another night, a badminton set. We put up the net and play badminton in the front yard all summer.

On the third night, I win a flashlight – a big, three-battery light with three switches so you can beam white, red, or green light. When we get home, we are walking from the garage across the driveway to the kitchen door. From the window of the back room upstairs, over the kitchen, Gertrude, who is living there and takes care of my baby brothers, calls down, "Did you win?"

I shine my new flashlight up at her, flicking from white light to red, then green, then back to white. When I climb into bed, my new flashlight is standing on its broad glass face on my bedside table. When I get up in the morning, my new flashlight is gone. I never see my new flashlight again.

# 15

## "There'll Be a Good Many Pairs of Shoes
## Bought for this Family."

Like the bank on the northwest corner, Tibbett's Jewelry on the northeast corner of Main and Bank is a solid rock holding down The Four Corners. The show window on the right of the door is always sparkling with silver: Revere bowls, gravy boats, serving dishes, table settings, candlesticks – everything a bride could dream of. The window on the left is filled with clocks and watches: ladies' delicate little wrist-watches with jeweled bands, men's with square faces and round faces and strong pigskin bands, men's pocket watches with heavy fobs, gold watch chains, cuff links and tie clasps, a tray of diamond engagement rings set in gold and silver, and, behind it all, mantel clocks in a row of brass and wooden mountings – in the center, my favorite: inside a bell jar, a small clock whose workings hitch back and forth with every tick.

I often linger at that window on the way home from school, checking to see if all the clocks and watches are telling the same time. If one or two have stopped, or do not agree, I want to go in and ask Mr. Tibbett, who is in there with his black hair

117

slicked down flat and his black necktie tucked into his white shirt between two buttons half way down his chest, if he knows. But I never have the nerve. Sometimes I daydream that he hires me as his official watch-setter.

The front door of Freeman's Drug Store is here on Main Street. Its windows are classic drugstore: tall, graceful bottles of colored water – red, green, blue – stand behind collections of brush-and-comb sets, shaving brushes, tiny bottles of perfume, larger bottles of after-shave. The north window, on the left, is loaded with school supplies: pencils, rulers, pencilboxes, notebooks. Inside, dark varnished cabinets rise to the ceiling behind the glass counters on each side.

The Freemans live on North Main, down just past the Erie Street corner and around the corner from Harold and Min Hawks. They, too, are childless. Soon they retire, selling the tall bottles of toilet water and everything with them to Alice Sayles, who has learned the business working in their store.

Next door, at Dan Dugan's Shoe Store, Dan Dugan's shoe salesman is always standing at the door as I walk home from school. He, too, is in white shirt and dark tie, with his sleeves rolled one fold back toward his elbows. His straight black hair is parted in the middle and slicked down, and his double chin folds out over his collar. A shoehorn is in one hand, and he slaps it against his other palm in front of his bulging stomach. His eyes follow me as I walk by. Sometimes Dan Dugan is standing behind him, taller, thinner, older, with wavy gray hair and steel-rimmed glasses and a serious look.

118

I do not know then what I later learn: Some years earlier, when Bill and I were three and four years old and Mama was writing up local news for the Buffalo and Rochester papers, Dan Dugan caught one of his clerks embezzling. He had to bring charges. But then he called Mama and asked her not to send the story to the papers.

"Why, Mr. Dugan," she said, "I can't do that. You've brought charges. That's news. I have to send it in."

It will be bad for business, he argued. He would lose customers if the story appeared. And then he threatened. He would make trouble for her. He would see that her work for the papers came to a halt.

That was when he learned that Mama was the original inventor of instant retort. "Mr. Dugan," she said, "you just go right ahead. There'll be a good many pairs of shoes bought for this family in the years to come. You just see how many come from your store."

As I look back at Dan Dugan's, I see me and my brother Bill, and then my brothers Hewitt and Leonard, who weren't yet born when Dan Dugan's was embezzled, trudging back and forth to school past that store, and I see Dan Dugan and his salesman silently watching us, growing boys with growing feet hiking past. Not once do we ever set foot inside the store.

## 16

### "You're the Original Forgotten Man."

A big yellow store stands beside the shoe store. It is still another grocery – the Market Basket. Like Meland's, it announces its specials and sales with white never-dry paint hand lettered high on the outside of the windows. And like Meland's and Flickinger's and Trippensee's and the three A & P's and D.B. Ryan's before them, it is a store where the ladies stand at the counter and recite their grocery lists while boys run here and there to collect the items.

Next door is The Four Corners' fourth drugstore, run by Bob Moore. Its paint is a rich butterscotch color, almost orange. Its windows concentrate on school supplies – notebooks, loose-leaf binders, pencil boxes, crayons, pencils, lined pads, erasers, pencil sharpeners. But the store disappears soon after Bob Moore commits suicide, in the early days of The Depression when I am in first grade. Mrs. Moore sets up a nursery school in their home – a big house with a broad front porch that comes out almost to the sidewalk and beige trim and shingles painted a deep blue-green (like no other house in town), at the corner of West Park and Clinton, just a block from

Blanche Beedon, whose husband took the same route out of The Depression the same year. Then in a couple of years she moves to the big farm at the town line on South Main – where her boys, who are already in high school, have room to spread. By the time Captain Boone flies his Navy Grumman to Albion a few years later, young Bob Moore and his brothers have learned to fly and have three or four Piper Cubs on the field and, out front on the edge of Route 98, a sign offering flying lessons and sight-seeing rides.

But meantime they invent. We get one of those winters – they come only once in 10 or 12 years – when the canal freezes solid without a snowfall and without strong winds to ripple the surface. Result: ice that is smooth as glass, and great skating for miles and miles, east or west. The Moore boys mount an airplane engine on the remains of what must have been a one-horse open sleigh. The big radial engine faces the rear, with a rudder set up behind it and controlled by ropes threaded through pulleys to a steering wheel in the center of the dashboard and facing the seat, which is wide enough for the driver and two passengers, in front. The engine mount stands on rods the boys have added to the structure, supporting its weight up from the long runners on the ice.

The rig is too big to go under the lift bridges, which are permanently in their down positions when the canal is closed for the winter. So the Moore boys slide it off their truck and onto the ice on the west side of the Main Street bridge. From there, the ice is theirs clear to Eagle Harbor, six miles away, where they must turn around before the next lift bridge.

121

They take passengers 25 cents a ride, two at a time, to Lattin's bridge (the first high bridge west). To the Gaines Basin Road bridge, 30 cents. All the way to Eagle Harbor and back, 50 cents. Mufflers are pulled up above coat collars, wrapping chins and noses and ears, for the engine is deafening and the wind can produce frostbite.

Bill and I are there to hear the roar and to see the skaters scatter as the Moore machine, shaking to the throb of the engine as if it wants to fly apart, starts to move. Then it smoothes out as the engine picks up speed, the propeller's blur becoming invisible, the whole contraption gliding toward the light band on the horizon of the gray late afternoon sky of Western New York. Bob Moore steers to the right and skaters – some so far away they seem not to move, yet they rearrange themselves on the left side of the silver track of ice where it curves southwest far beyond the State Highway Department depot – get out of the way.

When they come back, first we hear them – a hum, then a buzz. Now the engine's roar, as skaters move to the north side and Bob Moore, coming toward us, keeps to the right. Apparently some silent agreement to use the etiquette of the road has been reached. Now we hear the irregular cough of the idling engine as they glide to a stop only a few feet from the Main Street bridge. The Moore boys run over and push, their feet slipping on the ice, to turn the machine around so it is headed west again. The passengers, a man and woman I don't know, step off, pulling their mufflers from their faces, grinning. Eager replacements climb on.

Joe Donatelli's Barbershop is a tiny shop, just big enough for two barber chairs and four or five straight wooden chairs with their backs to the window. Joe is a big man with a heavy head of black hair down to his collar. He is all neck and shoulders in his white jacket.

When Mama gives me the five-string banjo that a Civil War veteran in Alabama gave her when she was a girl, Dad remembers that Joe Donatelli plays guitar and gives lessons. Maybe he can teach banjo, too. Joe comes to our house one evening with a new Beginner's Five-String Banjo book and starts to teach me tuning and chords. He seems to be studying the book himself as we go along. It is hard for me to understand everything he says in his heavy Italian accent. In the center of the cover of the book is pasted a square of white paper, cut a little lopsided. On it is penned the price: 75 cents. I lose interest in the lessons, and when Joe Donatelli is no longer coming around I scrape and peel the piece of paper off the cover. Beneath it is the printed price: 35 cents.

The Citizen's National Bank. Joe Donatelli's tiny barbershop hunches up against the big granite walls of the town's largest bank building. Across the sidewalk, at the curb, stands its clock: a square pillar topped, 12 feet up, by white round faces looking north and south, each two feet in diameter. You can tell the time from the corner of Main and Bank, half a block south, or from the canal bridge, half a block north. When I am checking the clocks and watches in the window of Tibbett's Jewelry, up at the corner, I always glance down the block to see what the Citizen's Bank clock has to say.

The big plate-glass windows on each side of the Citizen's Bank's double door are topped by fancy stained-glass insets – each a monogram script CNB in a circle, surrounded by flowers and leaves in graceful leaded curves. Inside are marble counters topped by the brass grills of teller cages. In the center, at the back, is the big walk-in vault.

The Citizen's National Bank is where Dad first worked after he graduated from Albany Law Schooll in 1912, before he went into the theatre. He was there to handle legal business, but often found himself in a teller's cage when things got busy or hands were short. He tells how, when he got there, he noticed an account that maintained a small balance. It was labeled with the middle names of the three officers who owned the bank. At the close of business each day, if the bank was short a few dollars or cents, they took from that special account whatever they needed to balance the books. And if the bank was over a bit, they made a deposit to the special account. "That way," said Dad, "they let everybody go home on time and never worried about a surprise visit from a bank inspector."

But the Citizen's Bank gets a surprise in 1933 when President Roosevelt closes the banks. Soon the Orleans Trust Company, at the corner of Main and Bank, takes over the Citizen's Bank. The big open lobby stands empty. The teller cages gather dust, their brass losing its shine.

Wally Dale, from Barre Center, takes over the building. The whole place turns white, inside and out. Bright fluorescent lights spread whiteness over aisles of shelving and bins of fruit and vegetables. Shopping carts roll. Check-out counters line up near the front door. The walk-in vault becomes the meat locker. "We didn't have to insulate it," Wally tells Dad. "The walls were so thick and solid, we just put in the coolers and hung the meathooks." Outside, high above the stained-glass CNB monograms, a sign as wide as the building proclaims DALE'S SUPERMARKET. The clock remains at curbside with new signs superimposed over the bank's name.

Soon the Market Basket, two doors away, closes up. After a while, a used furniture store replaces it. Wally Dale's bright new supermarket thrives.

One morning years earlier in 1932, in Rochester, Dad gets off the sleeper from New York and bumps into Wally Dale, who is just off the sleeper from Washington. Together they ride the early train to Albion. Wally tells Dad he has been down to the capital to see a man at the Reconstruction Finance Corporation to ask if he can get some help putting his canning factory at Barre Center back on its feet after the Depression hit (this is long before the fire that destroys it), and the R.F.C. guy tilts back in his chair and puts his hands behind his head and his feet on his desk and says, "Why, we don't have money for little companies like you, we're here to help the big corporations."

Wally says to Dad, "What can I do? Can't I go see my governor and do something about this?" and Dad says, "Why, certainly, go down to Albany and see Roosevelt." And that morning Dad makes a call to the Governor and Wally gets an appointment.

A few days later, Wally stops by to see Dad and tells him Roosevelt sent him to see a couple of banks in Rochester. And only a few days after that, Roosevelt, who is now running for President, makes his speech attacking the R.F.C. and the system that is helping the big corporations and he says it's "the forgotten man," the small businessman, who needs help the most. The phrase catches on and makes headlines, and soon Roosevelt is talking of "the forgotten man" in campaign speeches again and

125

again. When Dad runs into Wally Dale, he says, "Why, Wally, you're the original forgotten man."

## 17

### "Hello, Governor Roosevelt!"

When I think of Roosevelt, it is a summer morning and I am in the yard in front of our house. Tony Acri is there in his worn white overalls, with his hammer hanging from the loop below his right hip and his flexible ruler in its special pocket. He is measuring and sawing big planks. He assembles them into a broad ramp that rises from the edge of the driveway to the level of the porch, some six or seven steps above the ground and higher than my head. Dad has hired Tony to build the ramp because the Governor is coming.

The Governor arrives, a day or two after Tony Acri finishes the ramp, with a great wail of sirens from far off down Main Street. Motorcycles roar and throb into the south driveway and follow its horseshoe around behind the house, past Gertrude, who stands on the back porch holding the baby and calling, "Hello, Governor Roosevelt!" as the open touring car circles past the line full of diapers hanging there. (Afterward, a friend of my mother says, "Weren't you mortified to have the Roosevelts come in the wrong way and go round back past those diapers?" To which

Mama replies, "The Roosevelts have five children of their own. I reckon they've seen diapers before.")

He is a big man with two canes. He stands up in the open car and shuffles onto the running board, then onto the ramp built by Tony Acri. A young man, his son, steps beside him, and the Governor takes his son's arm and the son takes one cane. They move up the ramp slowly but steadily. Soon the Governor is sitting inside, in the big wing chair beside the fireplace, with a card table in front of him. We sit around him – Mama and Daddy and Mrs. Roosevelt and the son, whose name is Elliott, and Herb Reed (he is Orleans County Republican Chairman; my father is Orleans County Democratic Chairman) and Father Sullivan and Doctor Brodie and a great many others, and out on the porch Frank Mahoney, the butcher, is carving big hams for all the people on the lawn because Mama invited the entire town to "a buffet luncheon for the Governor," and Mama tells Gertrude to serve the hot biscuits now (Mama is from Alabama). The Governor is jolly.

But suddenly, just as he is about to dig into his plate of ham and potato salad and biscuits, he stops and looks around. "Why," he says, drawing out the word, "where's William?"

"I guess he went up to his room," says Mama. "You know, Governor Roosevelt, he's really an awfully shy boy."

The Governor puts down his knife and fork. "You just go tell him I won't eat one bite until he's here with me."

And he doesn't. Mama gets Bill (who is seven – I am five), and everybody makes room for Bill's plate on the card table in front of the Governor, and the meal

128

After ham and biscuits and before the speech: (l. to r.) Mama, Governor Roosevelt, Dad, Mrs. Roosevelt, with Bill (left) and Bernard. Photo by *Rochester Times-Union* or by *Rochester Democrat & Chronicle*.

proceeds. The Governor says things that make everybody laugh. He enjoys his lunch – especially the biscuits.

After lunch the Governor shuffles through the side door and out onto the porch. The photographers from the Rochester *Democrat and Chronicle* and the *Times-Union* want to take our pictures. We gather round as Elliott lets go of his father's arm and the Governor stands alone with his canes. The crowd is out in the front yard, but we are around here on the side because the side porch faces south and the light is better for the photographers (we are just where I am standing later when I watch Sambo bark a different bark to summon Prince to chase the stray dog, just where I watch the speeder kill Jiggs and hear him say he was hurrying to the dentist, and just above the steps where Walter Monacelli tells me how to ride a bike).

Bill and I and Mama and Daddy and Mrs. Roosevelt are in all the pictures. When my mother was getting ready for the Governor's visit, Terese McNall (mother of my pal, Tom) called her and asked if she wouldn't like her to "take the boys for the day" so we wouldn't be underfoot. Mama said, "Why, Terese, I wouldn't deprive them of that, they're part of the family and they'll be part of the event." So here we are, Bill and me in our white linen suits (short pants and matching tops) and Mama smiling up at the Governor and Dad very tall and proud and Mrs. Roosevelt smiling down at Bill and me, in a photo that hangs in my father's study, in the same house, for 49 years afterward.

After the picture-taking, the Governor shuffles along the porch to the front of the house and makes a speech to all the people on the lawn. It is a big lawn, big enough to play baseball and touch football on a few years later, and it is full of people. They have had ham and biscuits and potato salad. The next day, a friend of Mama's says, "My heavens, you don't mean to tell me you put heirloom silver out there on the tables for people to use? You had all those strangers in your yard using your silver? It's a wonder you have anything left." And Mama says, "Well, it never occurred to me not to. And I didn't lose a single piece."

Now the Governor moves slowly down the ramp, laughing and talking with those near him, and settles into the open touring car. Mrs. Roosevelt gets in, and Mama and Dad get in, and Bill and I get in, all of us in the back, which has extra seats that unfold out of the floor, and two state policemen get in the front seat, and two more stand on the running boards holding onto each end of the windshield, and the state police on their motorcycles start roaring and gunning their engines and off we go up Main Street and into town.

We ride to the "training school," as it is known around town. It is a women's penitentiary, officially called the New York State Training School for Women at Albion, and the Governor is including it on an inspection tour across the western end of the state. The school is a group of old red-brick buildings, with ugly rusting fire escapes, all separated widely by broad, well-shaded lawns. We pile out of the car. There is no ramp here for the Governor to step onto from his running board. He makes his way into some of the buildings. I find myself in another crowd, with my Aunt Holland and Uncle Tom and Cousin Eleanor, all of whom are visiting from Richmond, Virginia, and who were somewhere around the house during the buffet luncheon and now have turned up here at the training school. In the crowd, I am only slightly aware that the Governor is making another speech, has made another speech, has moved on. I am romping with Eleanor on the lawn under the tall shady trees, oblivious to the passage of time. Suddenly someone is shouting, "Here he is!" and I am gathered up, swooped up into a state trooper's arms and carried, utterly without dignity, to the Governor's car. All are aboard – the Governor, Mama and Dad, Mrs. Roosevelt, my brother Bill, and the state policemen. The trooper swings me over the side of the car and into the lap of my father on the jump seat. The sirens wail, the motorcycles roar, and off we go.

Now we are at the canal. The *Inspector* is waiting for us. It is the official yacht of the Governor, a big boat, I suppose 60 or 70 feet long. The Governor has come to Albion aboard it, though probably he didn't cross the entire state on it, since six miles an hour is the canal speed limit (lest you create a wake and break down the banks). We all get aboard. Aunt Holland and Uncle Tom and Cousin Eleanor show up and come aboard, too. We push off and people wave good-bye and bid us "Bon Voyage!" and we head west into the late afternoon sun. Governor Roosevelt is settled in a big wicker chair in the main cabin. Mama and Dad and Mrs. Roosevelt and Aunt Holland and Uncle Tom sit down in wicker chairs, too. They are all talking at once and having a grand time. I can tell that the Governor, just like my folks, loves to sit around and swap yarns.

Bill and I scramble all over that boat. We discover the engine room below decks, an open deck at the stern, a little deck atop the main cabin, and the staterooms up forward and down below in the stern. Cousin Eleanor is too shy to explore with us. She hangs around with the grown-ups.

We're out on top, up forward past where the man who is running the *Inspector* is in his little pilothouse. We can see one of the high bridges coming. These are the bridges by which the back country roads cross the canal. They are built high above the water, with the road climbing steeply up a big man-made abutment at each end. They are plain iron truss bridges with rattling plank floors. They look like something you made from an Erector Set.

The bridge we're approaching is the Gaines Basin Road bridge. A bunch of people are up there on the bridge, waiting for us to go under, and I recognize Gertrude. She has been relieved of duty at our house, has gone home (she lives up on West Bank Street, not far from the training school and not terribly far from the Gaines Basin Road). She has cut a huge bouquet from her mother's garden, and she is

132

lowering it to the *Inspector* on a long string. A man runs out of the pilothouse and grabs it. Gertrude calls down, "Hello, Governor Roosevelt!" the way she did from the back porch this morning, just as we glide under the bridge.

Bill and I hurry back into the cabin. The Roosevelts are both exclaiming over the flowers. The man says he'll find a vase and dip up some canal water for them. Mrs. Roosevelt jumps up and hurries out onto the little back deck. Gertrude and the others on the bridge have crossed to the other rail as we passed under them and are waving down to us. Mrs. Roosevelt raises her arm in a big wave and calls out, "Thank you! Thank you!"

When we get to Medina, the next town west on the canal, we pull up to the bank and all of our family get off. Someone has brought our car – the '28 Olds. We say our good-byes and thank the Governor and Mrs. Roosevelt for the ride. Dad takes the wheel and we drive back to Albion.


It happens all over again toward the end of the next summer. Tony Acri again builds the ramp, the state police again come in the wrong end of the driveway and escort the Governor the long way round behind the house and past the diapers (the baby of the first visit is my brother Hewitt, who is now seventeen months old, and the new baby, my brother Leonard, is now seven weeks old), Frank Mahoney carves the ham, somebody (not Gertrude, for she didn't last out the year) serves the biscuits, and the Governor makes a speech from the front porch. This time I am dimly aware that he is campaigning for reelection. And this time Mrs. Roosevelt goes upstairs to see the baby. She seems very tall as she stands beside the crib looking down at him.

133

The Governor has not come by boat this time, and when we all pile into the open touring car the police escort turns north and heads down Route 98 for Gaines, three miles away. At Gaines, we pull up to a big wooden platform like an outdoor stage. It is hung with red, white, and blue bunting. The platform is already crowded with people, sitting in four or five rows of chairs. The front row is empty, and we climb up (there is a ramp for the Governor) and sit down, my brother Bill and I just two seats away from the Governor and Mrs. Roosevelt, with Mama and Dad between us. The Governor is picking at a fingernail. Making his way up the ramp and pulling himself along by the rough two-by-four railing, he has run a big sliver under one nail. He keeps fussing with it.

We are looking out at the Ridge Road, which is the main highway between Rochester and Niagara Falls and was once an Indian trail and later the chief east-west stagecoach route in these parts. Between our platform and the road is a giant bulky something, half as big as an automobile, covered by a white canvas with an American flag tied over it.

The parade is headed by the American Legion color guard from the Sheret Post in Albion (a post that was organized by my father and was only the second or third to be started in New York state after the World War). The post band is right behind the color guard, followed by all kinds of fancy floats and exhibits mounted on farm trucks and tractors. Dr. Ben Howes comes along on horseback. Doc Howes is a veterinarian who lives down at Carlton Station, is in his seventies, and rides the nine miles each way into Albion any day the weather is good, which in summer is just about every day and in winter is almost never. We see him ride past our house nearly every afternoon, wearing the same outfit he's wearing now in the parade – red bandanna tied around his neck, plaid lumberjack shirt, knee britches and puttees instead of boots. He wears frameless spectacles and a full white beard. His face above the beard is well marked with liver spots. His horse prances and Doc Howes makes him step sideways past the reviewing stand as he doffs his broad-brimmed hat (not quite a cowboy hat, but almost) and waves to the Governor. Doc Howes rides as erect as a ramrod.

The best thing is the fresh-air taxicab. Amos 'n Andy are a household phrase, and the magazine ads for Pepsodent toothpaste have been doing something that radio left to the imagination – picturing the fresh-air taxicab that Amos drives. In the ads, which tell a story comic-strip fashion, the taxi is one of those cars that has a canvas roof over the front seat, where Amos drives, then a second windshield and a hard roof over the passenger compartment, with a second canvas roof over the back seat so that in fine weather the passenger can ride in the fresh air, too. And here comes Amos's fresh-air taxi in the parade, with two guys in blackface in the back seat, where the second roof is open. As in the magazine ads, the Amos at the wheel wears a dilapidated chauffeur's cap and the Andy beside him has derby hat and cigar. Just as the fresh-air taxicab arrives in front of the reviewing stand, it stops abruptly, like a wind-up toy automobile. It rears back on its haunches. The front wheels rise up in the air. The car balances precariously for a split second, the back seat swings like the seat of a Ferris Wheel, and the passengers are dumped backward into the middle of the Ridge Road. The front wheels drop to the ground, the seat falls back into place, and

135

Amos 'n Andy drive away, leaving their passengers to pick themselves up and chase off after them. The crowd is slapping its thighs.

More floats, more bands, and now the Legion band plays "Hail to the Chief," the crowd sings "America," the Girl Scouts recite the Salute to the Flag, the Boy Scouts recite the American's Creed, Frank Lattin welcomes the crowd, the band plays "America the Beautiful," and at last the Governor stands and shuffles to the podium to unveil the Historic Ridge Road marker. When the flag and canvas are pulled off, a giant boulder is revealed. On its face is a bronze plaque, and the words are read aloud:

Genesee to Niagara Historic Ridge Road

"I sing of the great Ridge Road,
Of the highway our children shall see,
Which lies like a belt on Ontario's shore,
Carved out in the wisdom of ages before,
For the races which yet are to be."

Trek – DeWitt Clinton – 1810

"In the great work of internal improvement
he persevered through good report and
through evil report with a steadiness of
purpose, that no obstacle could divert."

Erected by the
RIDGE ROAD IMPROVEMENT ASS'N
ORLEANS CHAPTER, D.A.R.
ORLEANS CO. PIONEER AND HISTORICAL ASS'N
STATE OF NEW YORK

This Marker is a Typical Specimen of Medina Sandstone
from the Noted Quarries of Orleans County Operated for
More Than a Century. Supply Practically Inexhaustible.


(It should be added in retrospect that, while the Supply of Medina Sandstone from the Noted Quarries of Orleans County was and is Practically Inexhaustible, the demand for the stone was not. For more than a century Medina Sandstone was barged down the canal to such cities as Syracuse, Schenectady, and Albany, and on down to the Hudson Valley cities and to New York, where it provided most of the curbstone as city streets were paved and most of the brownstone houses and brownstone churches built around the turn of the century. But the day of unveiling the Ridge Road marker is tragically close to the days when, despite the advertising plug cast in bronze

137

on the marker, all but a handful of the quarries become useful mostly as swimmin' holes, and dangerous ones at that, for the kids of the towns and farms near them.)

Following the Governor's speech, the band plays the "Battle Hymn of the Republic," the Reverend Mr. Pollock gives the benediction, and we all climb into the Governor's touring car and head east on the historic Ridge Road. When we reach the Monroe County line, the motorcycle escort slows to a halt, for the caravan is leaving the territory of the Orleans County Democratic Chairman. Again our car meets us and we say our good-byes and thank-you's and off we go. If a Monroe County Democratic Chairman is there with his wife and small boys to get into the Governor's car, I am not aware of it.

# 18

## "And I Won't See My Friends."

From these visits of the Roosevelts, I have the memory of the Governor as a dominating man, smiling, joking, boosting me into his lap when he sits in the big wing chair in front of the fireplace, friendly, asking about the town and the countryside he drives through, drinking it all in. I have the memory of Mrs. Roosevelt as tall and quiet, except when she hurries out on deck to wave to the receding bridge and call "Thank you! Thank you!" and when she goes upstairs to see the baby. Then she is warm and smiling.

The Governor becomes a face on a poster. Bill and I ride out from town with Dad on Saturday and Sunday afternoons all fall, nailing "Re-elect Governor Roosevelt" placards to tree and telephone pole. Mama takes me along sometimes when she goes canvassing in the farmland, and I sit in the car and watch her knock on doors and speak for a moment to the women who open them and then disappear inside for maybe three or four or five or sometimes as long as ten minutes. It is staunchly Republican country, Orleans County, so they are fighting a tough battle.

But maybe they have some effect, along with other workers in the party organization, for while 7,720 Republicans and 2,836 Democrats are enrolled, Roosevelt polls 3,709 votes out of 10,326 cast in 1930.

How did all this begin?

It started when Dad walked home for lunch one day from his office down at The Four Corners. He brought a letter from Mrs. Roosevelt. She and Mrs. Caroline O'Day, a Georgia woman interested in helping Franklin resume his political career after his recuperation from infantile paralysis, were planning a tour across the state to talk with Democratic women. She was writing to county chairmen, asking each to organize meetings.

"We'll not only have a meeting," said Mama, "we'll have a luncheon."

"Where?" said Dad.

"Right here. Where else?"

My father looked around. They were in the midst of having carpeting – installed years earlier – removed and hardwood floors put in over the broad-board subflooring. "In the middle of all this?"

"Certainly."

And so they did. And long afterward Mrs. Roosevelt told Mama that ours was the only home into which she was invited on that entire trip, that many of the county chairmen never even answered her letters, and that she never forgot just which ones had been so indifferent.

That first luncheon visit amid the torn-up floors goes back earlier than my memory. On another, Mrs. Roosevelt reached Albion by train in time for dinner at our house. Then Dad rushed her, late, to make a speech at the D.A.R. House down Main Street a way. After the speech, though they barely had time to make the train for Buffalo, Dad found his battery dead because he had left the parking lights on when he hurried into the D.A.R. House. He borrowed a car and Mrs. Roosevelt made the train.

Just before dinner one night, Mama calls Bill and me to her and says, "Now, when Daddy gets home tonight, you must say, 'Hello, Judge Ryan.'" Governor Roosevelt has appointed my father to a judgeship on the five-man New York State Court of Claims. The year is 1930, and it is the beginning of a 31-year career on the Court of Claims bench for Dad. (He is consecutively reappointed by Governors Lehman, Dewey, Harriman, and Rockefeller until he reaches the state's mandatory retirement age of 70.)

Mama and Dad celebrate Thanksgiving 1931 as guests of the Roosevelts at Warm Springs. While swimming in the warm water at Pine Mountain cottage, she and the governor talk about the Democratic convention scheduled for Chicago next June. Roosevelt says it will be important to have the Alabama delegation lined up for him because Alabama heads the list of states alphabetically and will be the first to vote for nominees.

"Don't you worry, Governor Roosevelt," says Mama. "You'll have Alabama."

"Why do you say that?" says the Governor.

"Because," says Mama, "my father will deliver the Alabama delegation."

Mama's father is William C. Fitts, a lawyer who, at age 28 in 1894, was elected attorney general of Alabama and who served as assistant attorney general of the U.S. during the Wilson administration. In March 1932 he goes from Birmingham to New York to visit Roosevelt headquarters, then announces that Alabama's 24 delegates to the convention will be for the Governor. "There is no doubt about that," he says. And on May 14 he visits Roosevelt at Warm Springs and assures him of the 24 Alabama votes.

Mama and Dad go out to Chicago at the end of June, Dad as delegate-at-large from New York State and Mama covering the women's side of the convention for the Rochester and Buffalo newspapers (both had gone to Houston in 1928 for the same purposes). They come home elated. They've seen their man nominated by a convention that stretched one session to 18 hours and four hard-fought ballots with Roosevelt ahead of Al Smith on each. They know his victory is thanks to the solid South and the Democrats' unit rule that makes all members of a state's delegation decide whom they want and then vote as one. They've been in the small group who went out to the airport to greet the Governor when he flew from Albany on July 3rd to break precedent as the first nominee to come to the convention to make his acceptance speech.

Now we're papering Orleans County with Roosevelt for President placards. Bill gets hold of a prize: a giant pencil portrait of the Governor, blown up onto a stretch of oilcloth six feet high by four feet wide, all stars and stripes and red, white, and blue around the edges and with the words "Roosevelt for President" across the top and "Vote Democratic" across the bottom. Bill figures out that this oilcloth poster will just fill his bedroom window. Our house has giant windows, big plate glass jobs, installed a generation before anybody invented the "picture window." Two of them downstairs are eight feet tall and six feet wide. Upstairs, in the front of the house, Bill's room and Mama and Dad's room each have big four-by-six-foot windows. Bill sees that the Roosevelt oilcloth not only just fits the window but is translucent, so he mounts a goose-neck desk lamp behind it and when you drive by after dark you see the biggest Roosevelt sign in Orleans County lighted in the upstairs window of Judge Ryan's house.

Inside, on his bedroom wall, Bill tacks up the Roosevelt for President and Lehman for Governor posters that we are nailing to every telephone pole. They stay on that wall for 45 years.

On the Friday evening before Election Day, 1932, Mrs. Roosevelt arrives after dark (held up in Medina by a jealous Democratic Town Committee chairman who purposely delays her in hopes of throwing her off schedule). Bill and I have been building a fancy soapbox racer, really more than a soapbox racer, with a wooden cart for a chassis and a body to rival those by Fisher of Detroit. More than merely something you put your legs inside and stick head and shoulders out of, it is all enclosed and roofed. We've covered its wooden frame with cardboard cartons

143

flattened out and tacked on, and added tin can headlights and a Model T's wooden steering wheel from Jake Rosen's junkyard. The car is ready in the garage behind the house when we hear Mrs. Roosevelt's sirens wailing and see the row of motorcycle headlights coming down Main Street. We rush into the garage and Bill gets inside and I push (Bill is customarily in command, while I usually provide the power) and as Mrs. Roosevelt's car pulls into the driveway we race into the glare of its headlights yelling, "Hello, Mrs. Roosevelt!" She stands there and ooh's and aah's and walks all around our car and says, "Isn't it wonderful!" and lets us know she has never seen anything quite so sensational.

Doctor Brodie is there for dinner. And Father Sullivan. And Herb Reed, for Mama is probably the only county chairman's wife in history who always includes the opposition chairman in her invitations to political luncheons and dinners. Maybe that helps account for the Roosevelt vote, too. Doctor Brodie is our family doctor. He brought us four boys into the world. Father Sullivan is actually Monsignor Francis J. Sullivan and he is an elderly man who has been very old and very deaf ever since I can remember (he makes people shout when he hears their confessions, then remembers what he is doing and pops out of the confessional and herds all who are waiting over to the far side of the church where he thinks they can't hear the loud confessions) and who remains just as elderly and just as deaf and never gets any older while I age 30 years before he eventually withers and dies. He is a man who created ecumenism before anybody invented the word. He spreads the joy of his being all over our small town, sharing the wealth of religion with all. He is an asset at any dinner table.

144

This time, the Rochester newspaper photographers are on hand once more. My brother Leonard is now big enough to talk and walk, though he doesn't yet talk very clearly, and we sit in the front room (like all big brick Victorian houses built in 1891, ours has two living rooms, one more relaxed than the other) on the small sofa in front of the portraits of Grandma Cochrane and Aunt Loolie (Mama's great-aunt, actually). Mama and Mrs. Roosevelt are seated on the sofa with Hewitt, Leonard, and me, and Bill and Dad stand behind us, and after the photographers have taken only one or two pictures Leonard jumps down and says, "I foo!" and marches out of the room. He can't be lured back for love nor money. When Leonard is foo, he is foo. Mrs. Roosevelt laughs and says, "Well, we certainly can't take any more pictures without him" and refuses to permit any more picture-taking.

Friday before Election Day, 1932, in front living room, just before Leonard said, "I foo" and departed. (Standing l. to r.) Dad and Bill. (Seated, l. to r.) Bernard, Mrs. Roosevelt, Leonard, Mama, Hewitt. Photo by *Rochester Times-Union* or by *Rochester Democrat & Chronicle*.

On this Friday evening, Mrs. Roosevelt again speaks at a reception at the D.A.R. house, with everyone and anyone in town invited if they're interested. Then she comes back to our house to stay, sleeping under the patchwork quilt handed down from Aunt Loolie, who was grown before the War Between the States.

Next morning, Mama and Dad drive her (no dead battery this time) half way to Syracuse, where a state car meets her. On the way, she says, "You know, Harriet, Franklin may very well win this election."

"Of course he's going to win," says Mama.

"You really think so?"

"I know it."

"Well, if he does, we'll have to move into the White House."

"You certainly will."

"And that's where I'll be. And I won't see my friends."

"Of course you will," says Mama.

"Harriet, I want you to promise me something." A pause. "Promise me you will never come to Washington without phoning me to say you're there. No matter what you think is going on. Will you promise me that?"

"All right. I promise."

On one visit, Mrs. Roosevelt brings us books. She gives Bill *The Boy's Book of Electricity*. She gives me a book she herself has written, titled *When You Grow Up to*

147

*Vote*. It has just been published (in 1932) and has short chapters that explain what all the people in government do, from the policeman and the fireman to the mayor and the governor. One of the illustrations shows a smiling policeman stopping traffic while two boys cross the street with their soapbox racer. The boy who is riding and steering could be Bill, and the boy who is pushing looks like me. Gazing back from today, I leaf through the book and wonder if Mrs. Roosevelt really wrote it, and then I read the first sentence of the one-page chapter titled "White Wings" ("The street cleaner is usually dressed in white and pushes a queer little cart in front of him") and I know that she did. Only an Eleanor Roosevelt of the 1932 period could let such description as "a queer little cart" suffice. The title page says the book is "By Eleanor Roosevelt (Mrs. Franklin D. Roosevelt)." Imagine some editor sitting there telling her they'll have to put her husband's name in so people will know who she is. On the flyleaf in her handwriting is the inscription, "To Bernard Ryan Jr. from a friend who happens to be the author Eleanor Roosevelt."

On election night, I go to bed in my room toward the rear of the house. Our big old house has a front stairway with two landing turns, a long hall down the center upstairs, and a back stair going down again to the pantry and kitchen. Soon after the Governor's victory is announced over the radio, the Sheret Post American Legion Band arrives at our doorstep. Playing "Happy Days Are Here Again" full blast, it marches in the front door, up the front stairs, down the hall past my bedroom, down the back stairs, through the kitchen, pantry, dining room, two living rooms and front hall and out the front door. I never wake up.

We're all invited to the Inauguration. Bill and I receive our own invitations, addressed to us in flowing calligraphy. We drive to Washington in the '30 Olds (Hewitt and Leonard are too little to go, but I am nine and Bill is ten going on eleven) and stay at the Mayflower Hotel. We have adjoining rooms with a bathroom between, and the lobby downstairs has columns and marble like a Roman bath. At the Capitol we sit directly in front of the inaugural platform, with the grandstand of news photographers behind us, looking straight up at the Governor and Charles Evans Hughes, who is the first man I've seen with a full beard since Doc Howes last rode by, as the Chief Justice administers the oath. I'm wearing my new blue serge suit, and Bill his new brown tweed, and we are both in knickers. Dad is wearing morning coat and trousers and his new silk hat, but he has to take off his hat when he gets into a taxi. It is bitter cold and the wind goes right through you.

In the reviewing stand, directly in front of the White House at the Inaugural Parade, we sit in the row just behind the President. The stand has white columns and pediments and some protection from the wind, but when you look up there is no roof. Hundreds of bands and soldiers and sailors march by, and floats from every state in the Union. Tom Mix rides past. He doesn't make his horse prance sideways like Doc Howes did. We are about frozen, and finally we leave when the sun, which looks warm but isn't, goes down and the parade is still going strong.

We go into the White House, and the Inaugural Reception is under way. Mrs. Roosevelt stands in the receiving line and says hello and calls us by name. We shake hands with about a thousand people and have tea and tiny cookies in the East Room.

After a while we shake hands all over again and go back to the Mayflower. We are still frozen.

We're getting ready to go to the Inaugural Ball. Dad is putting on his white tie and tails, and Mama has on a long glittery dress. Bill sighs and says, "I'm getting sick and tired of being introducted."

Every November, Mama bakes tons of Christmas fruitcakes from Grandma Cochrane's secret recipe. She sends them to all the folks down south, and to old friends everywhere. She's been sending them to the Governor's Mansion in Albany for four years, and now she sends one to the White House. "Mama," we say, "the Secret Service men are sure going to enjoy that fruitcake." But early in January comes a note from Mrs. Roosevelt telling Mama how they cut her fruitcake at a big family dinner and how much they all enjoyed it. And the fruitcake goes out and a note from Mrs. Roosevelt comes back every Christmas as long as Mrs. Roosevelt lives.

We are invited to the second Inauguration, on January 20, 1937. By now, my grandparents, Papa and Nonie, have moved from Birmingham to Washington, for Papa has become General Counsel to the R.F.C. (They had lived in Washington earlier, during the Wilson administration, when Papa was Assistant Attorney General.) Their home is on Ashmead Place, just off Connecticut Avenue and across the street from Congressman Hamilton Fish. When we're there visiting, I get to ride Hammy Fish's Irish Mail up and down Ashmead Place.

This time it is not windy and cold and dry. It is windy and cold and wet. The Inauguration is held in a wind-driven downpour. Our seats are in the same place, directly below the center of the inaugural platform, but nobody sits down. Everybody stands, some on the benches, trying to see past everybody else's umbrellas. We can't see Mrs. Roosevelt up there on the platform. She is late, and they seem to be holding things up for her. At last she appears and Roosevelt slips his hand into the glass case they have made to protect the Roosevelt family Bible from the rain, and he is sworn in. We pass up the Inaugural Parade to go back to Ashmead Place to dry out. I have never before seen a heavy overcoat and a blue serge suit soaked right through, but mine are. My shins are dyed blue from my suit. We hang our coats over the furnace down cellar and change everything we have on and, wearing still-damp coats, go off to the reception at the White House late in the afternoon and the Inaugural Ball that night. Mama says she thinks Mrs. Roosevelt was late for the swearing-in because she was running around trying to find us and get us up on the platform out of the rain.

Now whenever Mama goes to visit her folks, she calls Mrs. Roosevelt and, if Mrs. Roosevelt is in town, which is not always, Mama is invited to luncheon or to tea and a couple of days later, in her newspaper column "My Day," Mrs. Roosevelt mentions that she was there.

Mrs. Roosevelt is on the road a lot, and Mama and I have a way of turning up in her path. In March of 1938, we are in the railroad station at Springfield, Massachusetts, just changing trains, when we see a crowd of people and ask what's going on. "Mrs. Roosevelt is here – she's just arrived," says someone. We plant ourselves full in her path as she comes through the grand concourse, and Mama rushes up to her (probably knocking Secret Service men in all directions) saying, "Mrs. Roosevelt! Mrs. Roosevelt!" Mrs. Roosevelt embraces her, says, "Why,

Harriet, what are you doing here?" and I sweep off my hat and say, "Hello, Mrs. Roosevelt," and we chat for a few minutes and go our ways.

My parents never call the Roosevelts by their first names. He is always "the Governor" when referred to, and is addressed as "Governor Roosevelt," and she is always "Mrs. Roosevelt." But Mama and Dad are "Harriet" and "Bernard" to the Roosevelts. Mama remarks that the President likes to be called "the Governor" even after he is in the White House.

The convention is in Chicago again in 1940. Jim Farley hires Bill, who is now 18 and is about to enter Princeton in the fall, as a page working out of his office at the convention. Bill is, at least figuratively, at Farley's elbow during the split over the third term issue. He gets more than a taste of politics, and wants still more.

When the 1940 Inauguration comes, I am a student at Kent School, a boys' boarding school from which (at that time) it is impossible to escape for any reason less than a death in the family. But the Acting Headmaster, Father Chalmers (Headmaster Father Sill has recently had a stroke and is laid up) gives me permission to go, and plans are made. The day before I am to leave, Mama phones to say that Papa and Nonie both have the flu and we can't stay at their house, and, since it's impossible to get reservations at a hotel this late, we'll just have to cancel. I tell Father Chalmers, who is pleased that I am taking the disappointment like a good sport, and I miss the third Roosevelt Inauguration.

Three or four years later, while I'm a student at Princeton, some kind of *ad hoc* wartime political organization on the campus invites Mrs. Roosevelt to come speak, and darned if she doesn't accept. Tickets for Alexander Hall are distributed free, and a big dinner books the entire dining room of the Nassau Tavern, with Mrs. Roosevelt expected to arrive soon after lunch and spend the afternoon touring the campus and visiting with President and Mrs. Dodds. Mama has been in Washington and sends word that she'll come by to say hello to me on her way home. Without knowing it, she has picked the same day as Mrs. Roosevelt. So in the morning I heave into President Dodds's office and tell his secretary that I'm expecting my mother this afternoon and that she's an old friend of Mrs. Roosevelt and just happens to be coming along today and I wonder if maybe she can say hello to Mrs. Roosevelt this afternoon at the President's house or wherever. The secretary goes into Dodds's office, and I can hear their voices but can't quite make out what they're saying. Out she comes, an iceberg, and says Mrs. Roosevelt will be at the Nass just before dinner and "your mother can see her in the lobby." Instantly I am convinced that neither Dodds nor his secretary believes me. I thank her and get out.

At dinnertime, Mama and I and about 300 curiosity seekers are in the lobby of the Nass, jammed elbow to elbow. President Dodds comes in. Whispers say that Mrs. Roosevelt has gone to freshen up and will be getting off the elevator from the ground floor back, where the cars pull up, in a minute. Mama steps up to President Dodds and says she's Mrs. Ryan and her son called at his office this morning and she's known Mrs. Roosevelt for a number of years and had no idea she'd be in Princeton today but she's so glad she is and she wouldn't dream of being in town with her and

153

not saying hello. President Dodds looks uncomfortable (actually, he looks uncomfortable whether or not Mrs. Roosevelt and Mrs. Ryan are in town) and says she'll be here in a moment.

The elevator door opens. Mrs. Roosevelt moves into the lobby, taller than most people there. President Dodds says, "Mrs. Roosevelt, this is Mrs. – " and before he can get out the last word, Mama and Mrs. Roosevelt are in each other's arms and Mrs. Roosevelt is saying, "Why, Harriet, what are you doing here?" Then she turns to me, whom she hasn't seen since Springfield in 1938, and says, "Hello, Bernard."

In her speech to standing room only in Alexander Hall, Mrs. Roosevelt refers to the days when her husband was governor of New York and they crossed the state to visit the picturesque villages along the Erie Canal and inspect the state institutions in faraway places. The reference is so beautifully integrated into her address that no one would dream it is ad-libbed from the stirring of memory.

The fourth-term Inauguration is different. It is held in the back yard of the White House, with a crowd not larger than 300 or so on the lawn, looking up at the south portico that Truman later completes by adding a balcony. The President is pushed onto the portico in his wheelchair just as the ceremony begins. Two men lift him under his arms, stand him on his feet while he takes the oath of office, and let him down into the wheelchair again. His shoulders are more sloped than ever. His face is the gray of ashes. His eyes are deeper in his head and seem closer together than ever before, and the deep circles under them are dark brown. Mama says, "I've seen men that color before. He can't live very long, that color."

154

We go inside for a luncheon reception. Mama and Daddy are there, and Hewitt and Leonard, who was the baby Mrs. Roosevelt went upstairs to see when he was six weeks old. Bill, who was seven when he stood in the news photo on the porch, is in combat with the 32nd Division in the Philippines as a forward observer in the Field Artillery. The President is not at the luncheon. In the receiving line, Mrs. Roosevelt says he was just too tired to come. She introduces the unobtrusive-looking man beside her – Vice President Truman. We meet Faye Emerson, who has recently married Elliott. She catches people's names when she is introduced. There is no ball that night. When the East Room luncheon reception is over, the Inauguration is over.

On a Thursday in April, I ride my bicycle four miles through a balmy spring late afternoon from Princeton to Kingston to have dinner at Mike Potter's house. When I walk in, Mrs. Potter says, "Have you heard the news? The President is dead."

With a funny kind of feeling of personal possession, I see the nation perform the obsequies. I have grown up with the feeling that the leadership in government is not remote, is not impersonal, is not a mere figure. My feeling toward the men in the White House for all the years since then is governed by the thread of connection, thin and slight but somehow a connection, that I have had with the President since my earliest impression of a big open touring car and a jolly man who almost cannot walk.

Mrs. Roosevelt moves to New York and the United Nations, and when Mama and Dad are in the city they see her, maybe once or twice a year, sometimes more often, sometimes more seldom, for tea or for dinner in her apartment. My brother Bill returns from a year of occupation in Japan, finishes Princeton, earns his law degree at

155

Columbia, moves into Frank Hogan's office as an assistant District Attorney for New York County, which is Manhattan, lives on the Upper West Side in the Columbia neighborhood because his wife is attending Barnard, becomes active in politics, leads the Riverside Democrats in their reform fight against the Tammany-DeSapio machine, wins, finds himself District Leader in the 7th Assembly District, and in the spring of 1960 tackles the machine for keeps by putting on a primary fight for the nomination for the seat in Congress held by a DeSapio man in the 20th District.

Bill's organization holds a fund-raising cocktail party at the Park Sheraton Hotel. Adlai Stevenson and Eleanor Roosevelt are billed as guests of honor and speakers. I gather some Democratic friends from my office and go up at about four-thirty. The guests of honor have not yet arrived. I hang around the ballroom, where the party is being held, keeping half an eye on the lobby outside and the elevator doors. And suddenly my eye is caught by a tall figure in gray tweed, a fur piece of some sort around her neck. She is striding smoothly through the lobby, leaning forward as if walking into a gale, her pace brisk and effortless, a slight smile on her face. Bellhops and elevator men notice her, say something to each other about her, while she skims ebulliently and otherwise unnoticed through groups of guests in the outer lobby. Now she is in the precincts of the Ryan for Congress cocktail party, is greeted by the official greeters, moves on into the big room, talks quietly with Bill, listens attentively as he points out where they'll set up the receiving line in a moment. Suddenly Governor Stevenson appears as if by magic, the line is created, we who have come to see and listen queue up, and the party is in full swing.

When my place in the line at last reaches her, Mrs. Roosevelt looks at me, smiles, and says, without hesitation, "Hello, Bernard, how are you?"

It is 1962. Bill has served his first term in Congress. The regular Dems try again to beat down the insurgents by putting up another primary fight, and all over again Bill and the Reform Dems beat them and he gets the nomination. Having reached the mandatory retirement age of 70, Dad has retired from the New York State Court of Claims. He and Mama join the great number of enthusiasts canvassing the Upper West Side on Bill's behalf. Mama makes the Ansonia Hotel her special project, capturing the old-timers of opera and theatre who live there as 40 years earlier she captured the farm folks of Orleans County for her candidate. Then, the day before the election, she and Dad drive back upstate to cast their votes in the Town of Gaines and close up the empty big old brick house for the winter.

On Tuesday, November sixth, Bill wins again, and both his seat in Congress and the reform organization are secure. Next morning, I am in my office in midtown Manhattan. It is November seventh, the birthday of my elder daughter, Nora, and the birthday of her great-grandmother, Nonie, Mama's mother, for whom she is named. My phone rings and it is Mama, calling from Albion. I don't think she has ever before phoned me at the office.

"I've been thinking about Mrs. Roosevelt," she says. "You know, there's been a little squib in the paper the last few days, saying she isn't well."

Yes, I say, I've noticed it.

"Well, I meant to do something before we left New York. But I was so busy canvassing, I just never got to it. Could you call that florist around the corner from you? Or stop by at lunchtime? And have some flowers sent up?"

Sure, I say. I pull out my index-card box and look under "R." Here's the card.

"Maybe just send a dozen red roses. That would be nice. Let me give you the address."

I've got it right here, I say. 55 East 74th Street.

"That's it. Fine. Just put 'Love, Harriet and Bernard' on the card."

At lunchtime, I stop in at Marion Champol's on 45th Street. I make out the card, and she promises to send the roses up by mid-afternoon.

That evening, Nora is doing her homework in her room, with the radio on. Suddenly she is at the top of the stairs. "They just said Mrs. Roosevelt died early this evening in her apartment in New York."

I see flowers hanging from a string. The string is more than 40 years long. It stretches far, far across the breadth of New York State. And I see the tall figure sailing exuberantly through the crowded lobby, busily headed for a chance to help a young friend. She hurries to the place where she can stand waving up to the people on the bridge receding high overhead, and she calls, "Thank you! Thank you!"

# 19

## A Big Grin. A Big Wave.

On the north side of Wally Dale's Supermarket are three stores. One is called Woods & Sprague. The other is Woods & Vick. The two Woodses are brothers. The stores sell seed, flour, and feed – oats, barley, whatever horses and chickens eat – to the farmers of Orleans County. The stores are the downtown outlets of two big mills up on Washington Street by the railroad tracks, just past the depot. Each of the two tall silos of grain at the mills has one of the company names lettered on it.

I see the farmers come in on Saturday night, when all the stores downtown stay open until ten o'clock. They buy big sacks of flour and grain, so big they have to be trundled out across the sidewalk on dollies, then heaved up onto the front fenders of the Model T's, where they are cradled between the fender and the hood. Then the farm folks stand around the sidewalk and chat, the men in hats and suits with vests, the ladies in cotton dresses on a summer night. Once – maybe the Saturday night of an American Legion carnival, when parking at The Four Corners is especially tight because all of East Bank Street is closed off – we have to park on the north side of the canal, down past Kleindienst's Ford and Shelp's Chevrolet. We walk back up the slope to the Main Street bridge and over the canal, and I see sacks of grain or seed or flour on both front fenders of every car angled to the curb along the east side of Main – 12 or 14 cars in a row.

The Sprague of Woods & Sprague is Vernon B. Sprague. He is years and years ahead of his time. He invents a health food. In his mill, he processes a mix of whole-grain and enriched cereals and puts it in pale green packages labeled V-B-SAN. Maybe the V-B is for vitamin B and the SAN is for *sanitary* or some other healthy-sounding word, but we all know the name comes from the initials of Vernon B. Sprague, and we all know that V-B-SAN is good for you. Stacks of packages of V-B-SAN, each the size of a box of breakfast cereal, are on display in the window of Woods & Sprague.

Vernon Sprague himself needs health food. He is big around the middle, his stomach sagging out over his belt. His shirt collars always look too tight, his neck bulging out over them at the back, his double chin folding over the front. His hair is dark and thin and balding, combed slickly straight back. His wire-framed glasses cut into his nose and their temples plow across his cheeks to his ears.

The Spragues are among several friends of Mama and Dad who have built summer cottages at Rock Ledge, on the shore of Lake Ontario eight miles north of town. The only way to get to the cottages is a lane through the barnyard and pastures of farmer Henry Miles, who sold the folks the lakefront land. Henry Miles uses the lane, which is fenced on each side, to guide his dairy cows from one pasture to another, depending on where he wants them to graze, and he has a 12-foot-wide gate at the barnyard end and another a quarter mile away at the lakefront end. Each gate swings toward the south to open, back again north to close.

Those going to and from Rock Ledge must stop their cars at each gate and get out and open the gate, drive through, then get out and close the gate. All except Vernon B. Sprague. He discovers that the post of each gate is tilted just enough so that gravity will keep it closed without latching. So when he is headed south toward town and the mill and store in the morning, he bangs the bumper of his tan Pontiac into each gate, then scoots through as the gate swings wide, bounces against the lane's fencing, and settles behind him into its closed position. When Vernon B. Sprague returns in the evening, he has no choice but to stop at each gate, heave himself out of his car, open the gate, drive through, stop again, get out again, and close the gate.

Sometimes, whether it is Vernon Sprague or anyone else going through, the cows are in the lane and at the gate. That is when it gets tricky, seeing whether the car can get through without the cows deciding to get through. And that is why Vernon B. Sprague and others at Rock Ledge sometimes find meadow muffins on their lawns.

Upstairs over Woods & Sprague and Woods & Vick and the corner store is the *Orleans American.* Albion's third weekly newspaper, it is the one with the most news, for it carries columns about each of the hamlets and cross-roads communities around Albion: Childs, Gaines, Kent, Barre Center, Lyndonville, Waterport, Fancher, Kendall, Hulberton, Clarendon. The paper handles job printing, of course, and I stop in one time with Dad while he is getting NO HUNTING signs imprinted with his

161

name, for posting around the edge of our four acres. There is Bud Hart, who has recently finished college. They chat about Bud's plans. He is working as an editor, reporter, order-taker for job printing, whatever. But he doesn't plan to make the *Orleans American* his career. Within a few years, he is an editor at *Collier's Weekly* in New York, and later he spends many years as a senior editor at *Redbook*.

On the corner by the canal is Wilson's Hardware. The store window, trimmed in gray, bends around the corner with a tall pane of curved glass. It is the only window of its kind at The Four Corners. Inside are flashlights, pots and pans, trowels and spading forks and such garden tools, and beyond them two or three tables of electrical and plumbing parts. The store is dark. It seems to be an empty cavern back toward the rear, but light comes from a door to the right, far back. That is where my schoolmate Melvin Wilson and his mother and father live. Sometimes when you go into the store, you can smell what's for dinner. Often I stop in after walking with Melvin down Main Street from Central School, up beyond the Court House. But when I stop in, there never seem to be any customers.

Melvin and I are pals until, some time in first grade, he announces that they are moving. Where? To Palo Alto, California. I have never heard of it, but I like the sound of the name. Palo Alto. It never leaves me.

Now we are back at the Main Street bridge. On the east side here, the long stairway rises above three broad concrete steps. It stops high in the air, waiting for the bridge to rise to meet it, for the bridge is a "lift bridge" that goes up horizontally, staying flat and level so you can walk across while it is in the up position. Studying the stair, I think about the days when I am in Miss Duggan's fifth grade and I ride my bike to school every day.

I find myself in my brown corduroy knickers, pumping along from home down North Main Street. As I start up the slope toward the canal, I hear the three shrill toots of a tugboat asking the Main Street bridge to rise and let it through. If the toots are from the right, the tug is coming toward town from the west. And if it is pulling a long string of barges, I'm going to be standing beside the raised bridge and watching it go through – and I'll be late for school. Or I'm going to step on the gas – pump like mad – and ride two blocks east to cross the Ingersoll Street bridge before it goes up. Or I'm going to get off my bike and carry it up the long flight of steps to the raised bridge, ride across, and carry my bike down the long flight at the other end.

If I pump hard and hurry up the slope, maybe I can get across before the bridge starts to rise. But if the bridge operator answers quickly with his three replying blasts, I know the tug is too near and I won't make it. Usually I ride up to the top of the slope, where I can see beyond Kleindienst's Ford Garage and look along the canal.

Sometimes when I see that it is an especially long string of barges, bending into the distance with the curve of the canal out beyond the Highway Department's garages and gravel piles on the south side, I take a close look at the tugboat. It's ahead of the first barge by about 40 or 50 feet, with two taut heavy ropes stretched between. If the whole rig is moving more slowly than usual, I look at the flat roof of the tug's pilothouse.

163

Yes – there he is. Just clambering up the short ladder attached to the pilothouse. Now he's on the roof, standing erect. The tug has almost reached the bridge. As it passes under, the pilothouse clears the underbelly of the bridge by three or four feet. The man on the pilothouse raises his arms, grabs the girder below the bridge's guard-rail, lets himself be swept off the top of the pilothouse, pulls himself up so he can get one leg onto the edge of the girder, hoists himself over the railing, and starts running toward the stairs at the far end. I see him leap down the stairs two at a time. Now he's loping off past Wilson's Hardware and The Citizen's National Bank, dodging pedestrians. I know where he's headed. Of the three A & P's downtown, the one on East Bank Street is handiest, half way between Main and Ingersoll.

I jump onto my bike, zoom back down the slope from the bridge, race along Caroline Street parallel to the canal on the north side and pump up the slope to the Ingersoll Street bridge in time to hear the tugboat toot for that bridge to rise. Heart pounding, legs churning, I make it onto the Ingersoll Street bridge just as Joe McGuire steps into the center of the roadway with his STOP sign to halt the traffic, and up we rise.

I hurry to the railing facing west. Here comes the tugboat, slow and steady, its lines taut, its wake down to only a quiet bubbling, its barges barely rippling the water. In the bow of the tugboat, forward of the pilothouse, where there's a good-sized triangle of deck, a crewman is standing. He puts one foot up on the big capstan that's wound with rope, and leans forward, his elbow on his raised knee as he peers toward the corner of Bank and Ingersoll, a few yards from the bridge.

164

I look down to Bank from my perch at the railing on the raised bridge. Here he comes. More than a jog, but maybe not quite a hard run. How could he go any faster, I wonder, carrying those two huge brown paper bags of groceries?

He's around the corner, headed for the stair. He's up the stairs, two at a time, racing toward me. I back off, judging where the bow of the tug will pass under. He's there. Almost beside me. A big guy. Dungarees. A maroon sweatshirt with the sleeves cut off almost up to his shoulders. He could use a shave.

He drops the first bag of groceries into the arms of the waiting crewman, who sets it down, steps backward on the deck in one long stride, and catches the second bag just as it comes down. He disappears beneath us as I feel the hot air from the tug's stumpy smokestack.

My man is dashing across the bridge to the other railing. I drop my bike flat and follow. He swings himself over the railing in a single motion, steps down onto the girder below, grabs the lowest part of the rail, hangs a moment, legs dangling below the girder until the pilothouse comes out from under the bridge, and drops.

I stand at the railing as the tug moves away. My man is starting down the ladder on the pilothouse. He looks back at the bridge. He sees me. He grins. A big grin. He waves a big wave. I wave back.

I'm late for school. But Miss Duggan understands how hard it is for long strings of barges to be brought to a halt and tied up for shopping at The Four Corners.

Bill (right) and Bernard perched on the edge of the wide veranda, near the top of the south steps. Photo by Dad.

# Index

Freeman's Drug Store, 114, 118
Fuller, Ray, 29, 90, 94
Gaines Basin Road, 37, 122, 132
Gaines, New York, 134, 157, 161
Garrison, Arnold, 102
Garrison, Shorty, 102
Gminski, Richard, 18, 99
Great Atlantic & Pacific Tea Co., The (A & P), 28, 29, 86, 87, 112, 120, 164
Greyhound bus stop, 101
Grinnell, Gus, 85, 115
Grumman fighter plane, 45, 47, 48, 120
Gwenn, Edmund, 84
Hamlin, Mrs., 73
Harding, Earl, 44
Harding, Joan, 26
Harding, Marguerite, 26, 27
Harriman, Governor, 141
Harris Hill, 54, 57
Hart, Bud, 162
Hawks, Harold, 29, 30, 31, 48, 118
Hawks, Min, 29, 118
Hawks's Rexall Drugstore, 29, 32, 88, 90
Heard, Dick, 31, 32
    at Marsh's Hardware, 33
Heard, Donald, 31
Heard, Pete, 31
Heard, Tom, 17, 31, 32, 73
Hedges, Doc, 37-40, 43
Hengerer's department store, 84, 113
Hickey-Freeman, 25
Hogan, Frank, 156
Howard, Charlie, 82, 84
    Charles W. Howard Santa Claus School, 83-84
Howard, Father, 76
Howes, Doc, 134, 135, 149
Hubbell, Jimmie's Texaco, 94, 96,, 104
Hughes, Charles Evans, 149
International Order of Odd Fellows, 67-68
Kellogg & McCabe's newsstand, 113
Kelsey, Police Chief Horace, 94, 95, 96
Kent School, 152
King, Jennie, 103
Kirby, Tom, 91, 92, 93
Kleindienst's Ford, 159, 163
Krock, Arthur, 113

Kudner's, 113
Lake Ontario, 160
Landauer & Strauss, 26
Landauer, Jakey, 26, 28, 35
Lattin, Dr. Cora, 59
Lattin, Dr. Will, 59
Lattin, Frank, 136
Lehman, Governor, 141, 143
Lettis, Robert, 40, 41
"Little Orphan Annie" radio show, 46
Lonergan, Mrs. Jim, 111, 112
Lonergan, Jim, 111, 112
Macy's, 84
Magowan, Walter, 67
Mahoney, Frank, 128, 133
Marine Midland, 30
Market Basket, 120, 125
Marsh's Hardware, 33
Martina, Charlie, 61
McCurdy's, 113
McGuire, Joe, 79, 164
McKenna, Joe, 12
McMann Hotel, 77, 78, 79, 103
McNall and McNall Furniture, 49, 52, 58, 81, 85
McNall, Burt, 18, 50, 55, 56, 98
McNall, Terese, 52, 56, 130
McNall, Tom, 18, 49-53
Medina Sandstone, 23, 68, 73, 90, 137
Meland's IGA Market, 100, 101, 120
Merrill, Roy, 115
Merrill's Furniture, 49, 81, 85
"Miracle on 34th Street", 84
Miles family, 65, 66
Miles, Henry, 160
Miller, Marilyn, 29
Mix, Tom, 149
Monacelli, Albert, 75
Monacelli, Bill, 75
Monacelli, Carl, 75
Monacelli, Frank, 75, 114
Monacelli, Guido, 75
Monacelli, twins Rose and Elsie, 75
Monacelli, Walter, 18, 75, 129
Moore brothers, 121, 122
Moore farm
    Navy fighter plane on, 45
Moore, Mrs., nursery school, 120

## About the author

Bernard Ryan, Jr., has authored, co-authored, or ghostwritten 35 books in such topics as biography, early childhood education, community service for teens, career guides in the fields of advertising and journalism, court-room trials, and personal financial planning. His novel, *The Poodle at The Poodle*, which re-tells the Faustian legend in the setting of the advertising business in the 1960's, was greeted by *Publishers Weekly* as a "well-made book" that "offers great knowledge of advertising" and "descriptions of air travel . . . believable dialogue and a good hook." His *Tyler's Titanic* is an early chapter book about what happens when a boy finds a way to visit the wreckage of the great ship on the ocean floor. In *The Wright Brothers: Inventors of the Airplane*, he tells the sixth- to ninth-grade reader the Wrights' life stories and explains how they brought the world the miracle of flight. His *The Poisoned Life of Mrs. Maybrick* is the biography of an American woman who, in Liverpool, England, in 1889, was the defendant in one of history's great murder trials. Mr. Ryan has written many shorter pieces for magazine and newspaper publication and is a graduate of The Rectory School, Kent School, and Princeton University. A native of Albion, New York, he lives with his wife, Jean Bramwell Ryan, in Southbury, Connecticut. They have two daughters and two grandchildren.

172

6160464R0

Made in the USA
Charleston, SC
20 September 2010